(Highlights from)

The Gospel according to

Luke

Chapter 1 verses 1 to 4

To: My most excellent Theophilus
From: Dr. Luke
Subject: An orderly account of the things that have been accomplished amongst us.

Others before me have compiled a narrative based on the accounts of eye witnesses and ministers of the Word. And now, it seems good that I too should write, so that you may have certainty of the things that you have been taught.

highlights from **LUKE … chapter 1a**

1 DOWN: Zechariah was a priest during the time of H __ __ __ __, king of Judea. He and his wife Elizabeth were righteous people, but they were old and had no child. (Luke 1:5-7)

2 ACROSS: One day, when the people were praying outside the temple, and Zechariah was on duty burning incense inside the temple, an A __ __ __ __ appeared on the right side of the altar. (Luke 1:8-11)

3 DOWN: "Do not be afraid. The Lord has heard your prayer. E __ __ __ __ __ __ __ __ will bear a son and you will call him John; and he will turn many of the children of Israel to the Lord their God." (Luke 1:12-17)

4 ACROSS: Zechariah responded, "I am an old man, and my wife is advanced in years."; to which the angel answered, "I am G __ __ __ __ __ __, I stand in the presence of God. Because you did not believe you will be unable to speak until this is fulfilled." (Luke 1:18-20)

5 DOWN: The people waiting outside wondered what caused the delay in Zechariah's appearance. When he came out and was unable to S __ __ __ __ they realized that he had seen a vision. (Luke 1:21-23)

6 ACROSS: Zechariah returned home and Elizabeth became pregnant, and she remained inside for five M __ __ __ __ __. (Luke 1:24-25)

7 DOWN: In the sixth month God sent Gabriel, to Mary, a V __ __ __ __ __ who was betrothed to Joseph, and lived in Nazareth of Galilee. "Do not be afraid, Mary, for you have found favor with God." (Luke 1:26-30)

8 ACROSS: You will conceive and bear a S __ __ who you will call Jesus; He will be great and will be called the Son of the Most High. And the Lord God will give Him the throne of His father David, and He will reign over the house of Jacob forever, and of His kingdom there will be no end. (Luke 1:31-33)

9 DOWN: Mary answered, "H __ __ can this be since I am a virgin?" (Luke 1:34)

10 DOWN: Gabriel answered, "The Holy Spirit , and the power of the Most H __ __ __ will overshadow you; therefore the child will be called holy, the Son of God." (Luke 1:35)

11 ACROSS: "Your relative Elizabeth, in her old age, has also conceived a son. For N __ __ __ __ __ __ will be impossible with God." (Luke 1:36-37)

12 DOWN: And Mary said, "Behold, I am the servant of the L __ __ __; let it be to me according to your word." (Luke 1:38)

(To be continued …)

HEROD; ANGEL; ELIZABETH; GABRIEL; SPEAK;
MONTHS; VIRGIN; SON; HOW; HIGH; NOTHING; LORD

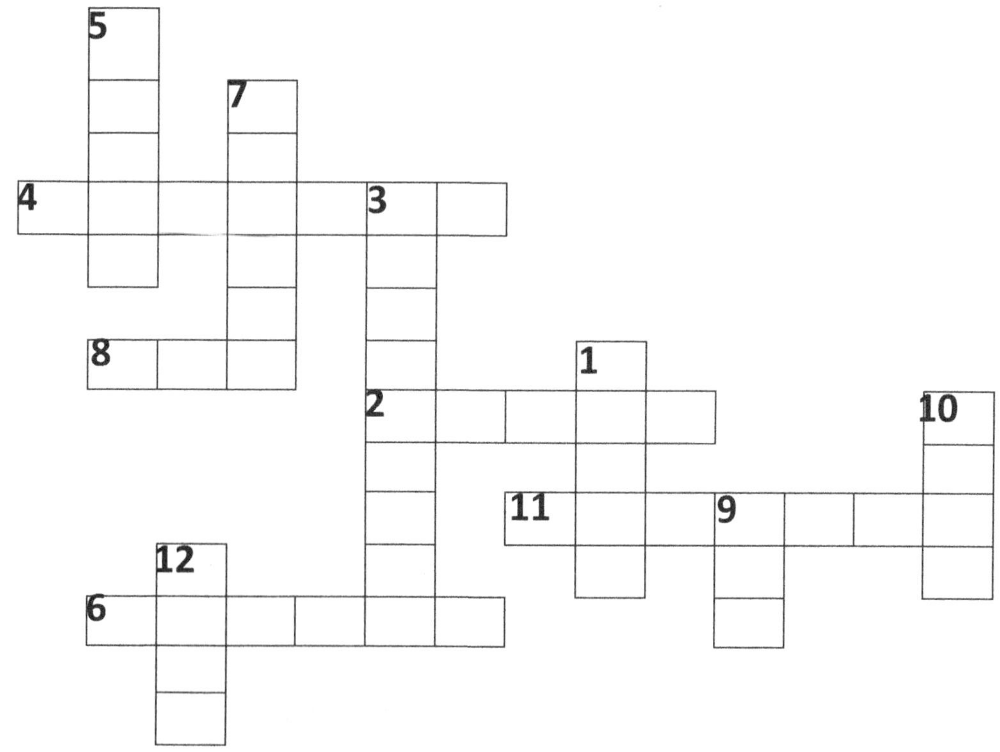

LUKE

Chapter 1a

Y W T R E S M O E I S T I U R F

C I H M T W T L L M T R A P M I

R S E O R C B T A E R E C N I S

E D R F I A E I I E V O B A H H

M O S T E L E A T S P T W T T E

R M S C V L G S R E F I P T O C

P H H A E E O G A P L I A I N A

G E N G L D O S P L N E Y S A R

P G I X I N D E M H R F D O O G

B W F A T H V D I G U P R C E N

C K L W H S L Q N V H O W H K E

A O G M T P U R J B M F T V S B

Luke, chapter 1 verse 32

He (Jesus) will be called great and will be called the Son of the Most High.

E G B U H Q M F I D C V J K N O
S U W X R E P P T Y B I Z F F G
M J G B L E S S E D K A N D T M
C P C P R V D G O B U R S V J U
R J O M D B N E H I S Z M Y P B
O E F Y O Z X L E A C A F J O F
P A V H G E Q V K M L V H R P A
T J O C N Y F T L F E W E Z B I
C X V I R K P B G U A D V U C W
K R D E T I S I V P J T R O F B
X J K V G R J P M U G N W Y J D
D N Y L S C T P I A L Q E U R H

Luke, chapter 1 verse 68

Blessed be the Lord God of Israel, for He has visited and redeemed his people.

highlights from **LUKE … chapter 1b**

1 DOWN: Mary then quickly left for Judea to visit Elizabeth. Elizabeth's baby leapt in her womb, as they G _ _ _ _ _ _ each other, and Elizabeth, filled with the Holy Spirit, exclaimed, "Blessed are you among women, and blessed is the fruit of your womb." (Luke 1:39-42)

2 ACROSS: Mary in turn responded, "My soul M _ _ _ _ _ _ _ _ the Lord, and my spirit rejoices in God, my Savior." Mary remained with Elizabeth for three months and then returned to her home. (Luke 1:43-26)

3 DOWN: Elizabeth gave birth, and on the eighth day at the time of his circumcision, the rejoicing relatives and friends, wanted him to be called Zechariah, after his F _ _ _ _ _. (Luke 1:57-61)

4 ACROSS: They appealed to Zechariah, when Elizabeth said that he should be called John. Then, Zechariah, asking for a tablet, since he could still not speak, W _ _ _ _ "His name is John". (Luke 1:62-63)

5 DOWN: Immediately he spoke, blessing God. All these things became the talk of all the hill country of Judea, saying, "What then shall this C _ _ _ _ be?" For the hand of the Lord was with him. (Luke 1:64-66)

6 ACROSS: Zechariah, then filled with the Holy S _ _ _ _ _, prophesied, "Blessed is the Lord God of Israel who, as spoken of from old by the prophets, has raised up a horn of salvation, that we should be saved from our enemies; … (Luke 1:67-71)

7 ACROSS: To show the M _ _ _ _ promised our fathers, the oath that he swore to our father Abraham, … (Luke 1:72-75)

8 DOWN: That we might serve him in holiness and righteousness all our days; and you child will be called the prophet of the Most High, for you will go before the Lord to prepare His W _ _ _. (Luke 1:76)

9 ACROSS: To give K _ _ _ _ _ _ _ _ of salvation to his people, in the forgiveness of their sins." (Luke 1:77)

10 DOWN: And the child grew, and became S _ _ _ _ _ in spirit, and he was in the wilderness until the day of his public appearance to Israel. (Luke 1:80)

(To be continued …)

GREETED; MAGNIFIES; FATHER; WROTE; CHILD;
SPIRIT; MERCY; WAYS; KNOWLEDGE; STRONG

LUKE

Chapter 1b

highlights from **LUKE ... chapter 2**

1 DOWN: Caesar Augustus decreed that all should be registered, so Joseph with his pregnant betrothed Mary, left for B __ __ __ __ __ __ __ __, the town of his lineage. (Luke 2:1-5)

2 ACROSS: There, she gave birth to her F __ __ __ __ __ __ __ __ son, wrapped Him in swaddling clothes, and laid him in a manger, because there was no room in the guest quarters. (Luke 2:6-7)

3 ACROSS: That night an angel appeared to S __ __ __ __ __ __ __ __, watching their flock, saying, “Fear not, I bring great, joyful news for all. A Savior, Christ the Lord, is born. As a sign you will find the baby wrapped in swaddling clothes, lying in a manger.” (Luke 2:8-12)

4 DOWN: Suddenly there was a multitude of angels praising God, “Glory to God in the Highest, and on earth P __ __ __ __ among those with whom he is pleased.” (Luke 2:13-14)

5 DOWN: The shepherds left and found Mary, Joseph, and the baby lying in a M __ __ __ __ __. All who heard of it marveled at what the shepherds told them; but Mary treasured all these things, pondering them in her heart. (Luke 2:15-19)

6 DOWN: At His circumcision, He was called Jesus, the name given by the angel before He was conceived. Simeon, a righteous, devout man, to whom The Holy Spirit had revealed that he would not die until he saw the Lord’s C __ __ __ __ __, came to the purification ceremony. Taking up the child Jesus in his arms, he blessed Mary and Joseph, saying, “This child is appointed for the fall and rise of many in Israel…”. (Luke 2:20-35)

7 ACROSS: Anna. An eighty-four-year-old widow, who was a prophetess in the temple also came, giving T __ __ __ __ __ to God and speaking of Him to all who were waiting for the redemption of Jerusalem. (Luke 2:36-38)

8 ACROSS: Jesus grew strong, filled with wisdom, and the favor of God was upon Him. When He was T __ __ __ __ __ years old, He went with His parents to the Passover feast in Jerusalem. (Luke 2:40-42)

9 ACROSS: On their journey back, they realized that Jesus was not with them or any of their relatives or acquaintances. They returned to Jerusalem, and after searching for three days found Him listening and asking questions of the teachers in the T __ __ __ __ __. He amazed all who heard Him, and astonished His parents. (Luke 2:43-48)

10 DOWN: “Your father and I have been searching for you in great distress”, His mother said. And He said, “Did you not know that I must be in my Father’s H __ __ __ __?” (Luke 2:49)

11 ACROSS: Jesus returned with them, and was submissive to them, and increased in wisdom, stature, and F __ __ __ __ with God and man. (Luke 2:50-52)

(To be continued …)

BETHLEHEM; FIRSTBORN; SHEPHERDS; PEACE; MANGER;
CHRIST; THANKS; TWELVE; TEMPLE; HOUSE; FAVOR

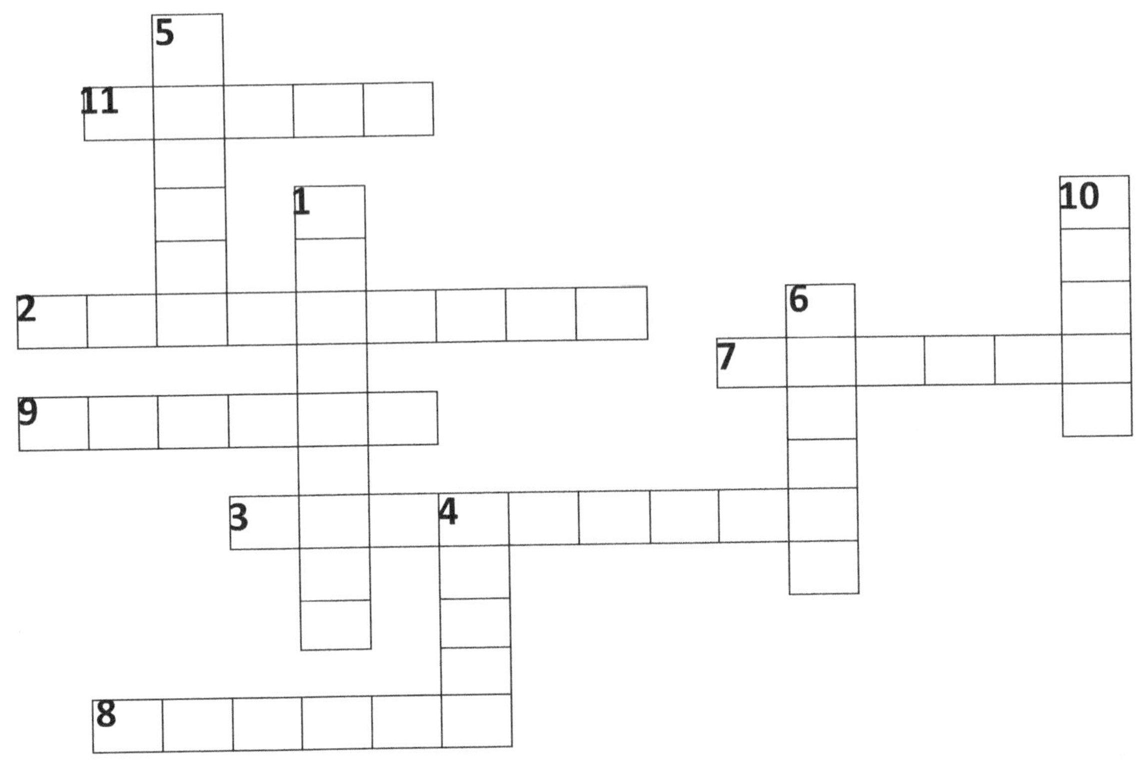

LUKE

Chapter 2

F	H	C	V	I	R	N	G	J	D	E	S	A	E	L	P
D	V	X	Y	D	E	Q	R	U	Z	A	B	K	G	E	H
N	N	H	C	F	W	L	I	M	P	L	J	O	A	U	N
D	F	A	R	S	E	I	H	Q	E	V	T	C	U	K	V
S	K	U	M	W	M	O	T	X	J	W	E	N	Z	Q	C
P	F	G	A	O	B	Y	M	H	B	D	B	G	K	P	G
M	B	Z	H	U	N	R	I	L	O	M	W	I	S	U	B
U	K	W	D	O	Z	G	U	M	H	S	X	F	A	D	J
D	F	P	J	S	H	L	J	H	V	B	E	W	V	O	W
L	S	F	N	E	T	O	C	W	H	K	U	E	P	G	C
Y	K	L	S	H	S	R	Q	N	V	H	O	W	A	K	E
E	O	T	M	T	F	Y	R	J	B	M	R	F	V	S	I

Luke, chapter 2 verse 14

Glory to God in the highest and on earth peace among those with whom he is pleased.

F H C V I R N G J F D C K L O P
K V X Y D E Q R U Z N B A G R H
N H T I W N L I M A L J S E U N
D F D R S E T H T E V T T U K V
S K U N W C O N X J G A I Z Q C
P I R E P E N T A N C E U K P G
M B W I U P R W I X M W R S U B
U K P D E Z G P M H I X F A C J
D F W R S L E J H V B S W V G W
L S F N D E Q C W H K U E P G C
Y K L W K S L Q N V H O R A E B
E O D M T F U R J B M R F V S I

Luke, chapter 3 verse 8a

Bear fruits in keeping with repentance.

highlights from **LUKE … chapter 3**

1 DOWN: It was the fifteenth year of Tiberius Caesar's reign; Pontius Pilate was governor of Judea; Herod was tetrarch of Galilee; his brother Philip was T _ _ _ _ _ _ _ of Iturea and Trachonitis; Lysanias was tetrarch of Abilene; and Annas and Caiaphas were high priests. (Luke 3:1-2)

2 ACROSS: The Word of God came to John in the W _ _ _ _ _ _ _ _ _, and he went into the region around the Jordan, proclaiming a baptism for the forgiveness of sins. (Luke 3:2-7)

3 DOWN: "Bear fruits in keeping with R _ _ _ _ _ _ _ _ _." He said, "Do not say to yourselves, we have Abraham as our father. For God is able to raise up children for Abraham." (Luke 3:8-9)

4 ACROSS: "What then shall we do?" they asked. John answered saying, "I B _ _ _ _ _ _ you with water, but He who is mightier than I is coming. He will baptize you with the Holy Spirit and fire." (Luke 3:10-17)

5 DOWN: So, with many other exhortations he preached good N _ _ _ to the people. (Luke 3:18)

6 ACROSS: But Herod, (who John had reproved about his brother Philip's wife amongst other evil things Herod had done) locked John up in P _ _ _ _ _. (Luke 3:19-20)

6 DOWN: At Jesus baptism by John, the heavens were opened and the Holy Spirit descended on Him like a dove; and a voice came from heaven, "You are my beloved Son; with You I am well P _ _ _ _ _ _". (Luke 3:21-22)

7 ACROSS: When Jesus began His M _ _ _ _ _ _ _, He was about thirty years old. (Luke 3:23)

8 ACROSS: He was assumed to be the son of Joseph; whose ancestry went back through Amos, Zerubbabel, David, Noah, Methuselah, and Seth, to A _ _ _, the son of God. (Luke 3:23-38)

(To be continued …)

TETRARCH; WILDERNESS; REPENTANCE; BAPTIZE;
NEWS; PRISON; PLEASED; MINISTRY; ADAM

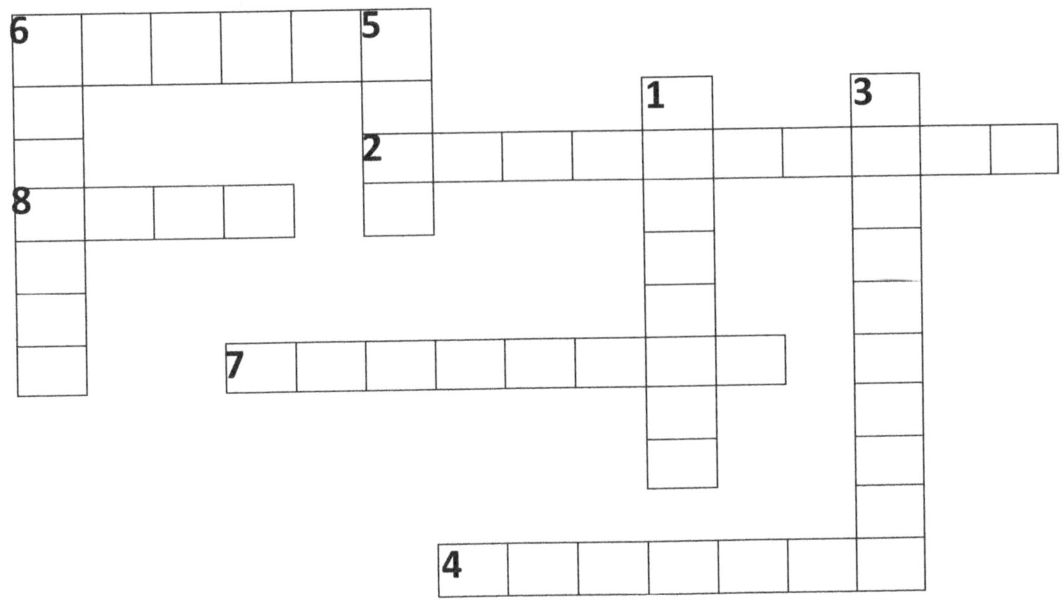

LUKE

Chapter 3

highlights from LUKE ... chapter 4

1 DOWN: Jesus returned from the Jordan, and was led by the Holy Spirit in the wilderness where he fasted for F __ __ __ __ days, and was hungry. The devil tempted Him saying, "If you are the Son of God, command this stone to become bread." (Luke 4:1-3)

2 ACROSS: Jesus answered, "It is written, 'Man shall not live by B __ __ __ __ alone, but by every word of God." (Luke 4:4)

3 DOWN: Then the devil in one moment showed him all the kingdoms of the W __ __ __ __ saying, "I'll give you all this authority and glory, if You will worship me." (Luke 4:1-5-7)

3 ACROSS: Jesus answered, "Get behind Me, Satan! For it is written, 'You shall W __ __ __ __ __ __ the Lord your God, and Him only you shall serve.' (Luke 4:8)

4 DOWN: Then the devil set Him on the pinnacle of the T __ __ __ __ __ in Jerusalem and said, "If You are the Son of God, throw yourself down from here for it is written 'He shall give His angels charge over you.'" (Luke 4:9-11).

5 ACROSS: Jesus said, "It is written, 'You shall not tempt the Lord your God.'" When the devil ended every T __ __ __ __ __ __ __ __ __, he departed until another time. (Luke 4:12-13)

6 ACROSS: Jesus returned to Galilee, preaching through all the surrounding C __ __ __ __ __ __, teaching in the synagogues, being glorified by all. In Nazareth, where He was brought up, He read from Isaiah on the Sabbath day, "The Spirit of the Lord is upon me, because He has anointed me to proclaim good news to the poor…" (Luke 4:14-19)

7 DOWN: All eyes were on Him as He began speaking, "Today this S __ __ __ __ __ __ __ __ has been fulfilled in Your hearing." They marveled at his words saying. "Is this not Joseph's son?" (Luke 4:20-22)

8 ACROSS: He said, "Truly, no prophet is acceptable in His hometown. Though many lepers were in Israel in Elisha's time, only Naaman the Syrian was cleansed." In anger they tried to T __ __ __ __ Him off the cliff, but he left, passing through their midst. (Luke 4:23-30)

9 DOWN: In the synagogue in Capernaum, a city in Galilee, Jesus rebuked the demon in a man: "Be S __ __ __ __ __ and come out of him". The people were amazed saying, "With authority and power he commands unclean spirits and they come out!" (Luke 4:31-37)

10 ACROSS: Next day, when he departed for a desolate place the people followed, but he told them, "I must preach the good N __ __ __ of the kingdom of God in other towns as well; for I was sent for this purpose." (Luke 4:38-44)

(To be continued …)

FORTY; BREAD; WORLD; WORSHIP; TEMPLE; TEMPTATION;
COUNTRY; SCRIPTURE; THROW; SILENT; NEWS

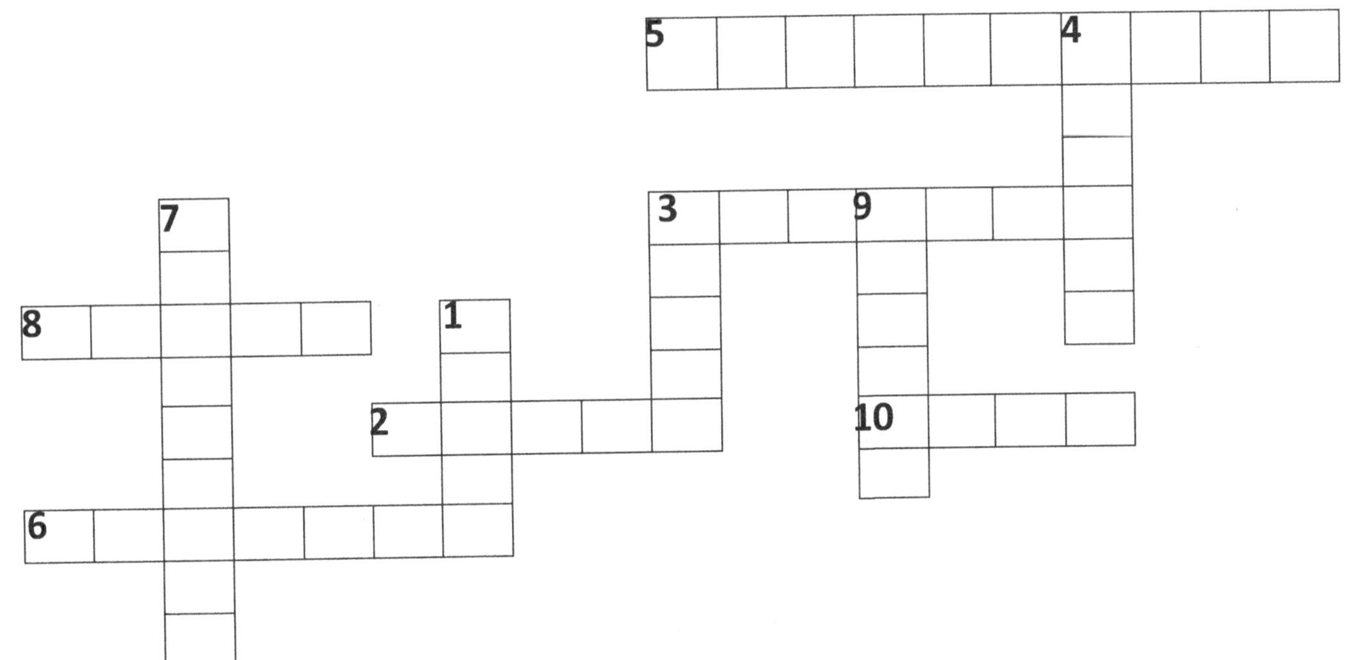

LUKE

Chapter 4

G W I R A E M T O I S D I U R F
S N H M T G C N H M T F A P M I
T D R O L P E V R E S E D N W S
E V L U X H H D A C T H R I U T
V O F A O W T Y A T V T A T O E
R E P C I Y G S B R N S E L Y C
E C I T E P K G A M H Y A I L A
S E H T H E D S P I N H P E N R
P L S O E N L L P H S F E D O G
B D R K T H V D I G U P R C R S
T I O U F P I Q L T F M V X I V
C M W K R B R O H Z K P D T P G

Luke, chapter 4 verse 8

You shall worship the Lord your God, and Him only shall you serve.

D F A H T R A E H C B U N T M N

R T V W B C O R A X A Z A E E F

M I F A D L J G K U J H M C O L

F O B P P C R F O C T Q U R I T

Q I S L U K M R V H W H G X O A

N D E F N Y W K E Z B I O I N Y

K Z N O S D P W J K V W Z R G Z

S I W B I A E S K E G V D Y I H

B N U H N J H R F O Z Q U T E T

J Q D L S X O A U T H O R I T Y

W I J U F P I Q L T F M V X I V

C M X K R B R O H Z K P D T P G

Luke, chapter 5 verse 24

But that you may know that the Son of Man
has authority on earth to forgive sins.

highlights from **LUKE ... chapter 5**

1 DOWN: Jesus standing by the lake of Gennesaret saw a crowd wanting to hear Him. He saw two boats, and getting into the one that belonged to S _ _ _ _ He put out a little from land, and taught the people. Afterward He told Simon to go out deeper and put down his nets for a catch. (Luke 5:1-4)

2 ACROSS: Simon answered Him, "Master, we toiled all night and took nothing! But at your word I will let down the N _ _ _". (Luke 5:5)

3 ACROSS: They caught such a large number of F _ _ _ that their nets were breaking. They signaled their partners in the other boat for help, and then both boats were so full that they began to sink. (Luke 5:6-7)

4 DOWN: Simon P _ _ _ _ fell down at Jesus knees. Those in his boat, and his partners, James and John, (Zebedee's sons) were astonished at the catch. (Luke 5:8-10)

5 ACROSS: Jesus said to Simon, "Do not be afraid, from now on you will be catching men."; and they brought their boats to land and then left E _ _ _ _ _ _ _ _ _ and followed Him. (Luke 5:10-11).

6 DOWN: A man with leprosy B _ _ _ _ _ Jesus to heal him; and Jesus touching him, immediately healed him. Report of Jesus spread even more; but He would withdraw to desolate places to pray. (Luke 5:12-16)

7 DOWN: One day as Jesus was T _ _ _ _ _ _ _ and healing, some men brought a paralyzed man on a bed. They had to let him down into the house, through a hole they made in the roof. Jesus seeing their faith said, "Man, your sins are forgiven you." (Luke 5:17-20)

8 ACROSS: The Pharisees and scribes questioned this, "This is blasphemy; who can forgive sins but God alone?" Jesus answered, "Which is easier to say, 'your sins are forgiven' or 'rise and walk'. The Son of Man has authority on earth to forgive sins." He then healed the man; and all around were amazed and glorified G _ _. (Luke 5:21-26)

9 ACROSS: After this Jesus called Levi the tax collector to follow Him. The Pharisees grumbled when they saw Jesus at Levi's house, but Jesus responded, "I have not come to call the righteous, but S _ _ _ _ _ _ to repentance." (Luke 5:27-32)

10 DOWN: They also questioned Jesus about why his D _ _ _ _ _ _ _ _ did not fast and pray like theirs and John's. Jesus responded, "The days will come, when the bridegroom is taken away from them, and then they will fast." (Luke 5:33-39)

(To be continued ...)

SIMON; NETS; FISH; PETER; EVERYTHING;
BEGGED; TEACHING; GOD; SINNERS; DISCIPLES

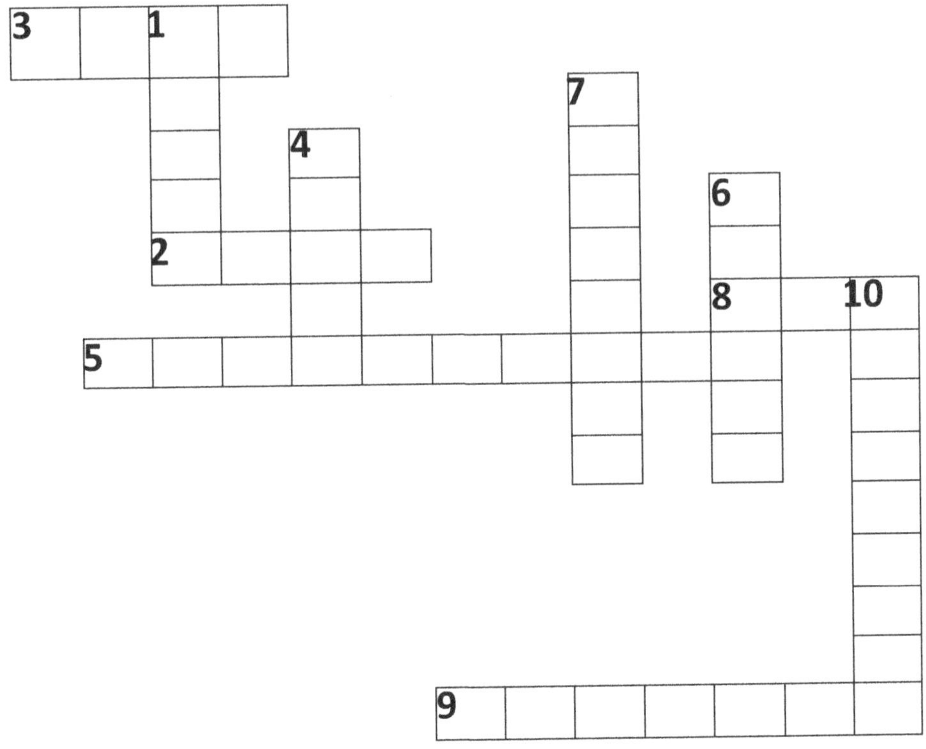

LUKE

Chapter 5

highlights from **LUKE … chapter 6a**

1 DOWN: One Sabbath, as Jesus and his disciples passed through a grainfield, the disciples plucked and ate some of the grain. The Pharisees questioned why they were doing what was unlawful on the S __ __ __ __ __ __. (Luke 6:1-2)

2 ACROSS: Jesus answered by reminding them that David, when he and his men were hungry, entered the temple and ate of the bread of the Presence, which was reserved for the P __ __ __ __ __ __. The Son of Man is Lord of the Sabbath. (Luke 6:3-5)

3 ACROSS: On another Sabbath, when Jesus was teaching in the S __ __ __ __ __ __ __ __, the scribes and Pharisees, watched Him, to see if He would heal the withered right hand of a man who was there. (Luke 6:6-7)

4 DOWN: Jesus knew what they were thinking. Calling them over he asked, "Is it L __ __ __ __ __ to do good or harm on the Sabbath?" He then healed the man's hand. The scribes and Pharisees were furious and discussed what they might do to Jesus. (Luke 6:8-11).

5 DOWN: Afterwards Jesus went to the mountains and prayed to God all night. Next day He chose twelve A __ __ __ __ __ __ __ from amongst His disciples: The brothers Simon Peter and Andrew; James and John; Philip, Bartholomew, Matthew, Thomas; James the son of Alphaeus; Simon the Zealot; Judas the son of James; and Judas Iscariot. (Luke 6:12-16)

6 ACROSS: A crowd of people from all over Judea, Jerusalem, Tyre and Sidon gathered to hear him and to be healed. He taught His disciples saying, "B __ __ __ __ __ __ are you poor, yours is the kingdom of God; you who are now hungry, you shall be satisfied; you who now weep, you shall laugh." (Luke 6:17-21)

7 ACROSS: "Blessed are you when people hate you, exclude, revile, and spurn you on account of the Son of Man! Rejoice, leap for joy, your reward is great in heaven; for so their fathers did to the P __ __ __ __ __ __ __." (Luke 6:22-23)

8 ACROSS: "Woe to you who are rich, you have received your comfort; W __ __ to you who are full, you shall be hungry; to you who now laugh, you shall mourn and weep. Woe to you when all people speak well of you, for so their fathers did to the false prophets." (Luke 6:24-26)

9 DOWN: "If you love those who L __ __ __ you, and if you do good to those who do good to you, and if you lend to those from whom you expect to receive, what credit is that? For even sinners do the same. Be merciful, even as your Father is merciful." (Luke 6:27-36)

(To be continued …)

SABBATH; PRIESTS; SYNAGOGUE; LAWFUL;
APOSTLES; BLESSED; PROPHETS; WOE; LOVE

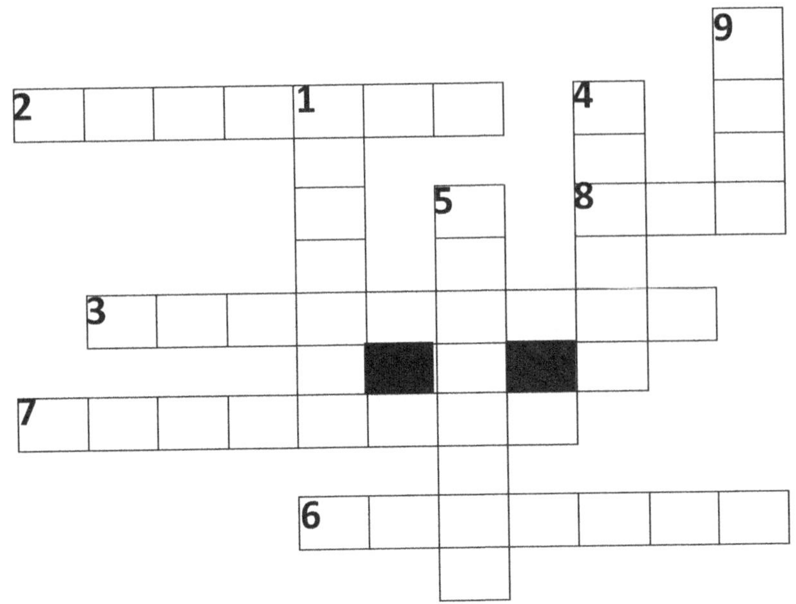

LUKE

Chapter 6a

E G B U H Q M F I D C V J K N O
S U D E N I A R T Y B A Z F F G
M J G B A M K H L O K I N D T M
C P C Q R D S L P D U R T V J U
R W T M V B U S W I V E M Y N B
O H F Y O F X L Y S A R F E O F
L A E K I L Q V K C L V H R P A
T J O C N B F J H I F W E Z B I
C X V I P K U E L P A R V U F W
K R E M H Y R T M L J T D O F B
X J K V G A B O V E I N W Y J D
D N Y L S C T N U A L W E U R H

Luke, chapter 6 verse 40

A disciple is not above his teacher but when he is fully trained will be like his teacher.

F H C S I R N G H E D W K H O P
E V I L D N Q E U Z A B A T R H
N K D C F E A I M P L S D U U N
D F O X P R O D U C E S T O K V
S K O N T U O T X C W A N M O C
P F G A P S Y M U B D B G K P G
M B W I U A R D L X M W I S U B
U K P D O E O U T H I S F A C J
D F W J S R T J H V B L I V E W
L S F N P T Q C W S K A E P S C
Y K L W H S L Q N V H O W A K E
M O D E T F U R J B M R F V S I

Luke, chapter 6 verse 45

The good person out of the good treasure of his heart produces good, and the evil person out of his evil treasure produces evil for out of the abundance of the heart his mouth speaks.

highlights from **LUKE … chapter 6b**

1 DOWN: Jesus continued to teach: "Judge and condemn not, and you will not be judged and condemned; give and F _ _ _ _ _ _, and it will be given to you and you will be forgiven. As you measure out, so it will be measured back to you." (Luke 6:37- 38)

2 ACROSS: He also told a parable: "Can a B _ _ _ _ man lead a blind man? Will they not both fall into a pit?" (Luke 6:39)

3 ACROSS: "A disciple is not above his T _ _ _ _ _ _, but everyone, when fully trained will be like his teacher." (Luke 6:40)

4 ACROSS: "Why do you see the speck in your brother's E _ _, but not notice the log in your own eye?" (Luke 6:41).

5 DOWN: "You hypocrite, first take the log out of your own eye, and then you will see more clearly to take out the S _ _ _ _ that is in your brother's eye." (Luke 6:42).

6 DOWN: "No good tree bears bad fruit, nor again does a bad tree bear good fruit. The good person, out of the good treasure of his heart, produces G _ _ _; and the evil person, out of the evil treasure of his heart, produces evil. Out of the abundance of the heart the mouth speaks." (Luke 6:43-45)

7 ACROSS: Jesus asked them, "Why do you call me Lord, Lord, and not do what I tell you? Everyone who hears my words and does them is like a man building a house who dug a deep foundation on the R _ _ _. "(Luke 6:46-48)

8 DOWN: "When the flood arose and the S _ _ _ _ _ broke, the house could not be shaken because it had been well built." (Luke 6:48)

9 ACROSS: "But the one who hears my words and does not do them is like a man who built a house on the ground without a foundation. When the stream broke, the H _ _ _ _ immediately fell and the ruin of the house was great." (Luke 6:49)

(To be continued …)

FORGIVE; BLIND; TEACHER; EYE; SPECK;
GOOD; ROCK; STREAM; HOUSE

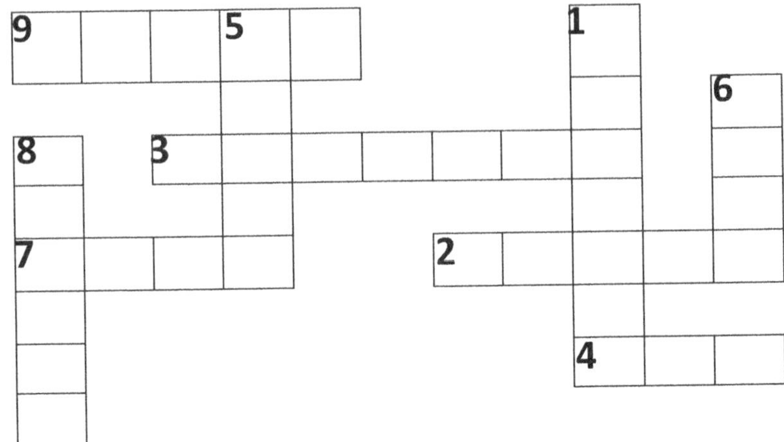

LUKE

Chapter 6b

highlights from **LUKE … chapter 7**

1 DOWN: Jesus went to Capernaum after speaking to the people. A C ___ ___ ___ ___ ___ ___ ___ ___ sent a delegation of Jewish elders to Jesus asking Him to come and heal his servant, who was terminally ill. (Luke 7:1-5)

2 ACROSS: On the way to the house, they met friends of the centurion bringing a message from him: "Lord I am not W ___ ___ ___ ___ ___ to have you come under my roof. But say the word and let my servant be healed. For I too am a man set under authority, with soldiers under me; and I say to one 'Do this, and he does it.'" (Luke 7:6-8)

3 DOWN: Jesus marveled at him, and turning to the crowd following Him said, "I tell you, not even in Israel have I found such F ___ ___ ___ ___." When the friends who had been sent returned to the centurion's house, they found the servant well. (Luke 7:9-10)

4 DOWN: Soon after this Jesus, accompanied by His disciples and a great crowd, went to Nain. Near the town's gate, they saw a great crowd accompanying a W ___ ___ ___ ___, as they carried her only son for burial. (Luke 7:10-12)

5 ACROSS: The Lord compassionately said to her, "Do not weep."; and touching the bier said, "Young man, I say to you arise." He arose, and fear seized all and they glorified God. This report of Him spread through all the S ___ ___ ___ ___ ___ ___ ___ ___ ___ ___ ___ ___ country. (Luke 7:13-17)

6 DOWN: John the Baptist sent two of his disciples to Jesus asking, "Are you the One, or shall we look for A ___ ___ ___ ___ ___ ___ ___?" Jesus replied, "Go tell John what you have seen and heard." "I tell you none is greater than John. Yet the one who is least in the kingdom of God is greater than he." (Luke 7:18-28)

7 ACROSS: To the scribes and Pharisees listening He said, "John the Baptist came eating no bread and drinking no wine, and you say, 'He has a D ___ ___ ___ ___'; the Son of Man has come eating and drinking and you say, 'Look at Him, a glutton and a drunkard'. Yet wisdom is justified by all her children." (Luke 7:29-35)

8 DOWN: A Pharisee named Simon invited Jesus to his house. While there, reclining at the table a known sinful woman of the city, washed his F ___ ___ ___with her tears, dried them with her hair, and anointed them with ointment from an alabaster flask. Responding to Simon's challenge, Jesus told of two men forgiven of debts; one $500 and the other $50. (Luke 7:36-42)

9 ACROSS: Jesus asked Simon which would love the moneylender more. Simon responded the one with the larger D ___ ___ ___. "Therefore", Jesus responded "Her sins which are many are forgiven, for she loved much." And to the woman He said, "Your faith has saved you, go in peace." (Luke 7:42-49)

(To be continued …)

CENTURION; WORTHY; FAITH; WIDOW;
SURROUNDING; ANOTHER; DEMON; FEET; DEBT

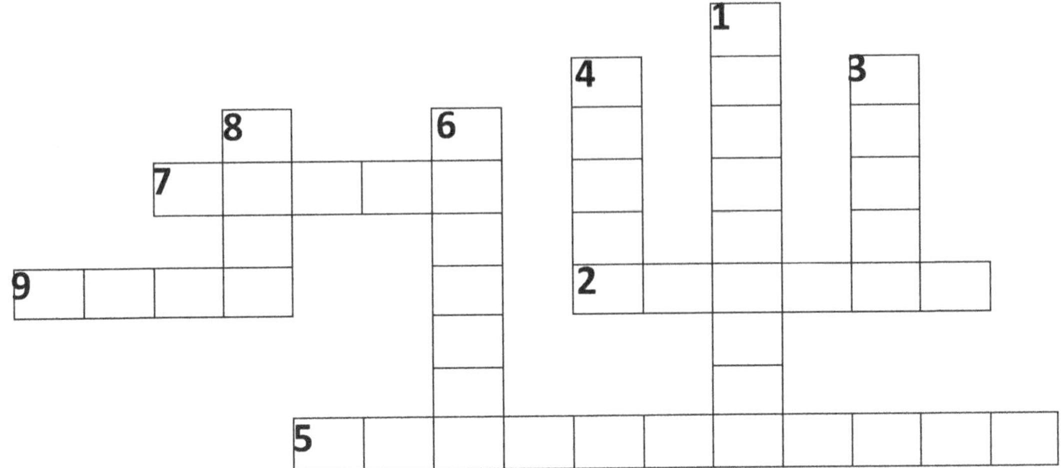

LUKE

Chapter 7

Y W T R E S M O E I S T I U R F

C I H M T W T L L M T R A P M I

R S E O R C B T A E R E D N I S

E D R F N A E I L E V O B L T P

M O S T E L M A L S P T W T H E

R M S C R O G S R E F I P Y O C

P H H A D E I F I T S U J B N A

G E N S L D O S P L N E Y S A R

P G I X I N D E M H R F D O O G

B W F A H R V D I G U P R C E N

C K L W C S L Q N V H O W H K E

A O G M T P U R J B M F T V S B

Luke, chapter 7 verse 35

Yet wisdom is justified by all her children.

A	D	F	R	E	S	M	O	E	P	S	T	X	U	R	F
C	I	H	M	T	W	T	F	L	M	T	R	A	P	M	I
R	S	E	O	R	C	B	T	A	E	R	E	C	N	J	S
E	Y	R	F	I	B	E	I	P	Z	V	O	B	A	F	H
M	O	T	H	E	R	C	A	D	S	P	T	W	S	T	E
R	A	S	C	V	O	H	S	R	E	F	K	P	O	X	C
P	N	B	A	U	T	O	G	A	P	L	V	A	I	R	A
G	D	R	A	E	H	B	S	J	L	Y	E	N	S	A	D
P	K	I	X	I	E	C	E	M	H	R	F	D	O	G	J
B	W	F	A	Q	R	V	D	I	G	U	P	R	C	E	N
C	N	L	W	H	S	L	Q	N	V	H	O	W	H	K	Y
X	O	G	M	T	P	U	R	J	A	M	F	T	V	S	B

Luke, chapter 8 verse 21

But He (Jesus) answered them, "My mother and my brothers are those who hear the Word of God and do it."

highlights from **LUKE … chapter 8a**

1 DOWN: Jesus and the twelve went through cities and villages preaching the good news of the kingdom of God. Some W __ __ __ __ who had been healed of evil spirits and infirmities went with them: Mary Magdalene, Joanna wife of Herod's household manager, Susanna and others. (Luke 8:1-3)

2 ACROSS: As people gathered, He spoke a P __ __ __ __ __ __ of a farmer who scattered seed. Some falling on the pathway was trampled and eaten by birds; others on rock with no moisture quickly withered away; others among thorns that choked them as they grew; and others on good soil, growing and producing a hundredfold. (Luke 8:3-8)

3 DOWN: When the D __ __ __ __ __ __ __ __ asked what the parable meant Jesus said, "To you it has been given to know the secrets of the kingdom of God, but for others they are in parables so that, 'seeing they may not see, and hearing they may not understand.'" (Luke 8:9-10)

4 ACROSS: Then Jesus explained. "The seed is the W __ __ __ of God. The path represents those who hear but the Devil takes it from their hearts so they may not believe. The rock, those who hear and receive the Word but grow no roots so in time of testing they fall away." (Luke 8:9-12)

5 DOWN: "The T __ __ __ __ __ are the cares, riches, and pleasures of life that choke some, and their fruit does not mature. And the good soil, those who hear, hold fast and bear fruit with patience." (Luke 8:13-15)

6 DOWN: Jesus continued teaching: "No one lights a lamp and then H __ __ __ __ it; but puts it on a stand so others may see the light. Take care how you hear, for to the one who has, more will be given; and from the one who has not, even what he thinks he has will be taken away." (Luke 8:16-18)

7 ACROSS: When Jesus was told that his mother and brothers were trying to reach Him through the C __ __ __ __, he responded, "My mother and my brother are those who hear the word of God and do it." (Luke 8:19-21)

8 DOWN: One day Jesus and his disciples got into a B __ __ __ to go across the lake. As they crossed Jesus fell asleep and while He slept a storm brewed, filling the boat with water. Feeling that they would perish they woke Jesus, and He rebuked the winds and the waves, asking them, "Where is your faith?" (Luke 8:22-25)

9 DOWN: They marveled, saying to one another, "Who is this, that He commands even winds and water, and they O __ __ __ Him?" (Luke 8:25)

(To be continued …)

WOMEN; PARABLE; DISCIPLES; WORD;
THORNS; HIDES; CROWD; BOAT; OBEY

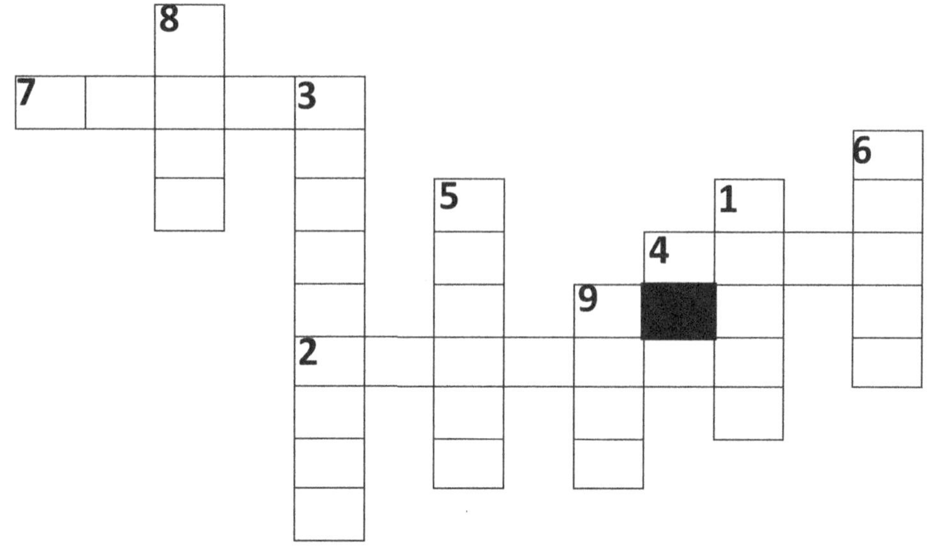

LUKE

Chapter 8a

highlights from **LUKE ... chapter 8b**

1 DOWN: Jesus and the disciples sailed on to the Gerasenes' country, opposite Galilee. There a demon possessed man who used to walk N ___ ___ ___ ___ amongst the tombs approached Jesus, falling down before Him shouting, "What have you to do with me Jesus, Son of the Most High God? I beg you, do not torment me." For Jesus had commanded the unclean spirit to come out of the man. (Luke 8:26-28)

2 ACROSS: Jesus then asked him, "What is your name?" And he said, "Legion", because M ___ ___ ___ demons had entered him. and they begged Him not to command them to depart into the abyss. (Luke 8:30)

3 DOWN: With Jesus P ___ ___ ___ ___ ___ ___ ___ ___ ___, they came out of the man and entered the pigs on the nearby hillside, whereupon the herd rushed down the steep bank into the lake and drowned. When the pigs' herdsmen told the townspeople, they went and saw the man, sitting at Jesus feet, clothed and in his right mind. Seized with fear, all the people asked Jesus to depart from them, so He got into the boat to return. (Luke 8:31-37)

4 ACROSS: The healed man, begged Jesus that he might stay with Him but Jesus sent him away saying, "R ___ ___ ___ ___ ___ to your home, and declare how much God has done for you." (Luke 8:38-39)

5 DOWN: When Jesus returned a crowd welcomed him. Jairus, a ruler of the synagogue came imploring Him to come to his house and heal his twelve-year-old D ___ ___ ___ ___ ___ ___ ___ who was dying. (Luke 8:40-41)

6 DOWN: A woman who had been hemorrhaging for twelve years was in the crowd. Though she had spent all her money, no doctor had helped her. When she touched the fringe of His garment the bleeding I ___ ___ ___ ___ ___ ___ ___ ___ ___ ___ stopped. (Luke 8:42-44)

7 ACROSS: Jesus perceived that healing power had gone out from Him and said, "Someone touched me." Trembling, the woman spoke up; and Jesus on hearing her story said to her, "Daughter, your F ___ ___ ___ ___ has made you well; go in peace." (Luke 8:245-48)

8 ACROSS: While Jesus was speaking someone came from Jairus' house with the report that his daughter had died. But Jesus said, "Do not fear; only B ___ ___ ___ ___ ___ ___, and she will be well." (Luke 8:49-50)

9 DOWN: At the house Jesus entered with only Peter, James, John and her parents. Though all were W ___ ___ ___ ___ ___ ___and mourning, Jesus said, "She is not dead but sleeping" and took her by the hand saying, "Child, arise." (Luke 8:51-55)

10 DOWN: Her P ___ ___ ___ ___ ___ ___ were amazed for she arose, and ate the food offered her; but Jesus charged them to tell no one what had happened. (Luke 8:56)

(To be continued ...)

NAKED; MANY; PERMISSION; RETURN; DAUGHTER;
IMMEDIATELY; FAITH; BELIEVE; WEEPING; PARENTS

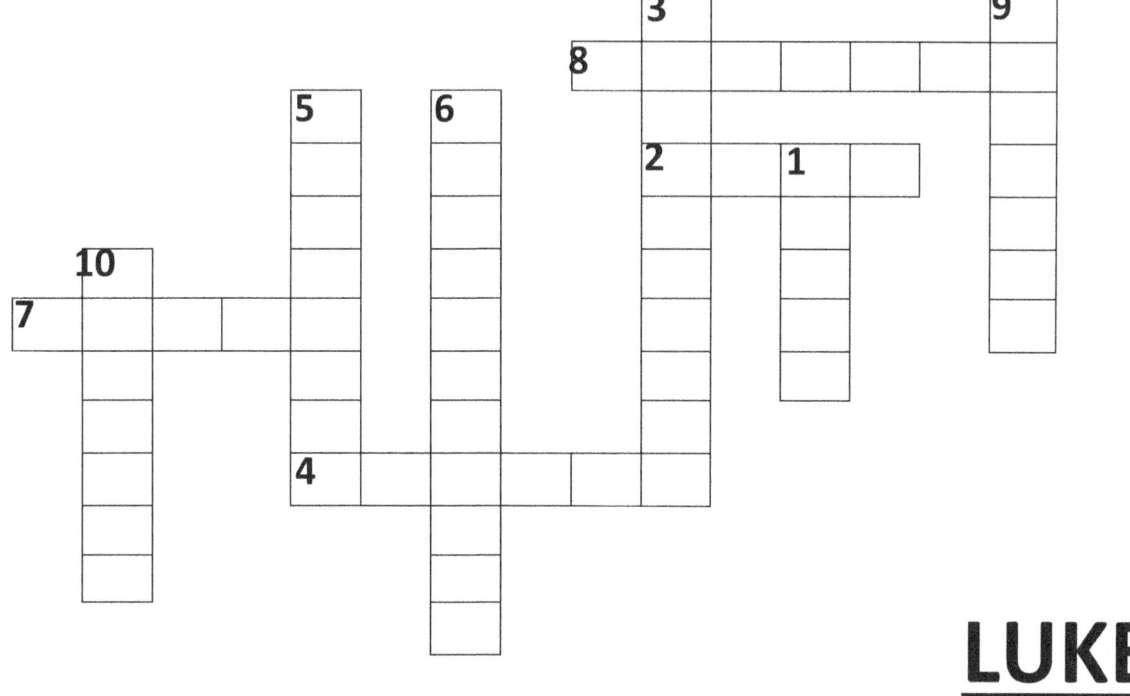

LUKE

Chapter 8b

F	N	I	R	A	E	M	D	A	I	S	D	I	U	R	G
I	Y	H	M	T	G	C	O	H	M	T	F	B	P	M	S
T	O	D	A	L	V	L	N	U	E	R	A	D	N	W	P
E	W	R	E	S	H	J	E	A	C	I	Q	R	U	I	K
V	B	F	A	C	W	T	Y	F	H	V	J	V	T	L	H
R	Q	L	C	O	L	G	S	B	R	N	S	E	L	O	C
E	D	A	H	B	P	A	C	A	U	O	Y	A	I	N	U
S	E	C	T	R	E	D	R	P	I	N	H	P	E	W	M
P	L	S	O	G	N	M	L	E	H	S	F	K	D	O	G
B	W	F	K	T	H	V	D	I	G	U	P	R	C	R	S
N	I	J	U	F	P	I	Q	L	T	F	M	V	X	I	W
C	M	X	K	R	B	R	O	H	Z	K	P	D	T	P	G

Luke, chapter 8 verse 21

Declare how much God has done for you.

D	F	A	Q	G	R	L	E	H	C	D	U	I	J	M	N
R	T	V	W	B	E	O	F	S	E	N	O	Y	N	A	F
M	A	F	A	D	T	J	G	S	N	J	N	M	C	L	S
H	I	M	S	E	F	Q	I	O	C	E	Q	R	E	I	T
Q	O	S	A	U	A	R	L	R	D	W	Y	S	X	O	A
N	D	E	X	N	E	W	K	C	Z	L	M	L	Q	N	K
K	Z	U	G	S	D	P	W	J	V	I	W	Z	I	G	E
S	I	N	B	M	X	E	S	K	H	G	V	D	Y	A	H
B	W	U	H	Q	J	R	H	F	T	Z	Q	U	T	E	D
J	Q	D	L	G	X	P	A	U	H	I	S	C	N	Y	A
W	E	J	U	F	W	O	L	L	O	F	M	V	X	I	V
C	M	E	K	R	B	R	O	H	Z	K	P	D	T	P	G

Luke, chapter 9 verse 23

Then He said to them all, "If anyone desires to come after Me, let him deny himself, take up his cross daily and follow Me.

highlights from LUKE ... chapter 9a

1 DOWN: Jesus sent the twelve out to proclaim the K __ __ __ __ __ __ of God and to heal. He told them to take no staff, bag, bread, money or spare tunic; to stay the whole-time at the house they enter and if a town does not receive them, to "shake the dust from your feet as a testimony against them." (Luke 9:1-6)

2 ACROSS: Herod the tetrarch, who beheaded John the Baptist, was perplexed by all that he heard; for some people were saying John was raised from the dead, and others said Elijah or one of the P __ __ __ __ __ __ __ from old had risen. (Luke 9:7-9)

3 DOWN: After the apostles returned, reporting all that they had done, Jesus withdrew with them to Bethsaida but the crowds followed. Jesus welcomed them and spoke to them of the kingdom of heaven and C __ __ __ __ those in need of healing. (Luke 9:10-11)

4 DOWN: At evening the twelve wanted to send the crowds away to find lodging and food, but Jesus told them to give them something to eat. They declared that they had only five loaves and two F __ __ __ for about five thousand men. (Luke 9:12-14)

5 ACROSS: Jesus, looking up to H __ __ __ __ __ said a blessing, broke the loaves and fish and had the disciples distribute them to the crowd. All ate and were satisfied and twelve baskets of leftovers were picked up. (Luke 9:15-17)

6 DOWN: When Jesus asked the disciples who the crowds said He was, they answered John the Baptist, E __ __ __ __ __ or one of the other prophets. "But who do you say I am?" He asked, and Peter replied, "The Christ of God." Jesus told them to tell no one saying, "The Son of Man must be rejected, killed and on the third day be raised." (Luke 9:18-22)

7 ACROSS: Jesus went on to say to them, "If anyone would come after me, let him deny himself and take up his cross daily and follow me. For whoever would save his life will lose it, but whoever loses his L __ __ __ for my sake will save it." (Luke 9:23-24)

8 DOWN: For what does it profit a man if he gains the W __ __ __ __ world and loses or forfeits himself. (Luke 9:23-27)

9 ACROSS: About eight days later, Jesus took Peter, James and John up the mountain to pray. While there His face appeared altered and his clothes became dazzling white; and Moses and Elijah appeared and spoke. As they were leaving Peter said, "Master, it is G __ __ __ for us to be here; let us make three tents ..." (Luke 9:28-33)

10 DOWN: As he spoke they were overshadowed by a C __ __ __ __, and a voice was heard saying, "This is my Son, my Chosen One; listen to Him." And then Jesus was found alone. At that time, they told no one what happened. (Luke 9:34-36)

(To be continued ...)

KINGDOM; PROPHETS; CURED; FISH; HEAVEN;
ELIJAH; LIFE; WHOLE; GOOD; CLOUD

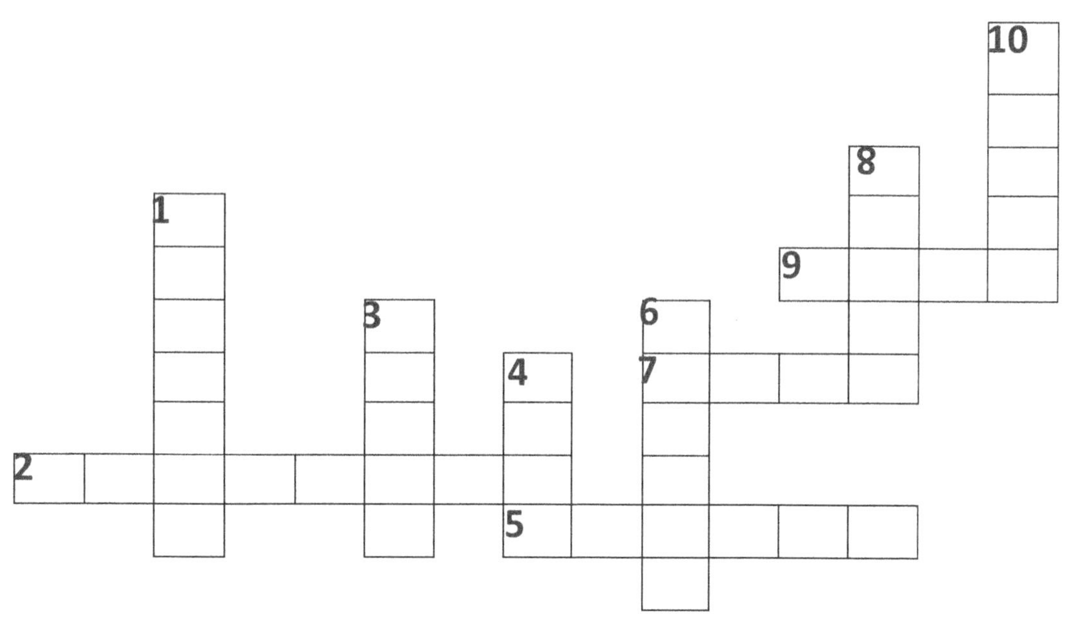

LUKE

Chapter 9a

highlights from **LUKE … chapter 9b**

1 ACROSS: It was the day after Jesus' transfiguration and a man in the crowd begged him to heal his only son who had a spirit which would seize him, convulsing him so that he foamed at the M ___ ___ ___ ___. He had already begged the disciples to heal him, but they were unable to do so. (Luke 9:37-40)

2 DOWN: Jesus responded, "O faithless and twisted generation, how long am I to be with you and bear with you? Bring your son here." And Jesus R ___ ___ ___ ___ ___ ___ the unclean spirit and healed the boy; and all were astonished at the majesty of God. (Luke 9:41-43)

3 ACROSS: While they were marveling at this, Jesus said to his disciples, "Let these W ___ ___ ___ ___ sink in: The Son of Man is about to be delivered into the hands of men." But they didn't really understand and were afraid to ask what He meant. (Luke 9:44-45)

4 ACROSS: An A ___ ___ ___ ___ ___ ___ ___ arose amongst them as to who was the greatest. Jesus taking a child to His side said, "Whoever receives this child in my name receives me, and whoever receives me receives Him who sent me. For he who is least among you is the one who is great." (Luke 9:46-48)

5 DOWN: Then John said, "Master, someone who does not F ___ ___ ___ ___ ___ us was casting out demons in your name, so we tried to stop him." But Jesus said, "Do not stop him; the one who is not against you is for you." (Luke 9:49-50)

6 DOWN: As the time approached for Him to be taken up, Jesus determined to go to Jerusalem, and sent messengers ahead to make preparations. They entered a Samaritan village but when the people there realized His destination was J ___ ___ ___ ___ ___ ___ ___ ___, they would not receive Him. (Luke 9:51-53)

7 ACROSS: James and John wanted to C ___ ___ ___ down fire from heaven to consume them, but Jesus rebuked them, and they went on to another village. Luke 9:54-56)

8 ACROSS: As they continued on the road, someone said to Jesus, "I will follow you wherever you go." Jesus said to him, "Foxes have holes, and birds have N ___ ___ ___ ___, but the Son of Man has nowhere to lay His head." (Luke 9:57-58)

9 DOWN: To another Jesus said, "Follow Me." But he responded, "Lord let me first go and bury my F ___ ___ ___ ___ ___." To which Jesus said, "Leave the dead to bury their own dead. As for you, go and proclaim the kingdom of God." (Luke 9:59-60)

10 ACROSS: And yet another said, "I will follow you Lord, but let me F ___ ___ ___ ___ say farewell to those at my home." Jesus said to him, "No one who puts his hand to the plow and looks back is fit for the kingdom of God." (Luke 9:61-62)

(To be continued …)

MOUTH; REBUKED; WORDS; ARGUMENT; FOLLOW;
JERUSALEM; CALL; NESTS; FATHER; FIRST

LUKE

Chapter 9b

E G B U H Q M F I Y C V J K N O

S U W X C D P P T D B A R O F N

M J G B A C K L O O K S N D T E

C P C Q R D S G P I U R S V J U

R H E A V E N B N D V D M Y P B

O S F Y O Z X G Y A C N T J I F

L D V H T E D V K W L A H R P A

T J N C N O F T L O H W E Z B I

C X V A M K S I G U A R V U F W

K R E M H Y P B V P J T D O F B

X J K V G R J P M U G N W Y J D

D N Y W W O L P I A L Q E U R H

Luke, chapter 9 verse 62

No one who puts his hand to the plow and looks back is fit for the kingdom of God.

A	Z	B	Y	H	X	D	W	E	V	F	U	D	T	H	S
I	R	J	Q	K	P	J	O	M	N	S	H	A	Z	D	W
B	O	I	Y	O	U	R	S	E	L	F	T	G	A	R	N
R	B	O	V	C	V	U	Q	H	E	A	R	T	U	K	V
S	H	U	N	W	C	O	T	J	F	W	S	N	Z	S	C
P	G	D	A	P	B	Y	M	E	B	G	U	F	T	P	G
M	I	W	I	U	F	R	W	L	X	M	O	R	K	U	B
U	E	P	Z	O	Z	H	U	M	H	I	E	D	A	C	J
G	N	W	J	P	T	E	D	O	V	N	L	Q	V	F	P
L	O	V	E	I	G	Q	C	W	G	D	U	E	P	G	C
L	K	L	W	H	S	L	Q	T	V	N	O	W	A	K	E
A	O	G	M	T	P	U	H	J	B	A	S	F	V	S	B

Luke, chapter 10 verse 27

You shall love the Lord your God with all your heart, with all your soul, with all your strength and with all your mind and your neighbor as yourself.

highlights from LUKE ... chapter 10

1 ACROSS: Next the Lord sent out S __ __ __ __ __ __ more disciples, in pairs, to heal the sick and preach the kingdom of God in the places He was about to visit. He said to them, "The harvest is plenty but the laborers are few; pray for the Lord to send laborers into His harvest." (Luke 10:1-2)

2 DOWN: "Behold I send you out as lambs among wolves. Carry no money bag, sack, or sandals and greet no one along the road. When you enter a house say, 'P __ __ __ __to this household' and do not go from house to house if they receive you." (Luke 10:3-9)

3 DOWN: "If a city does not receive you go into its streets and say, 'We wipe off the dust of your city that clings to our feet; but know that the kingdom of God has come N __ __ __ to you.'; It will be more tolerable in that Day for Sodom, than for that city." (Luke 10:10-12)

4 ACROSS: The seventy returned with joy saying, "Lord even demons are subject to us in Your name." Jesus replied, "Rather R __ __ __ __ __ __ because your names are written in heaven." (Luke 10:17-20)

5 ACROSS: Then Jesus rejoicing in the Spirit, praised His heavenly Father saying, "It seemed good in Your sight to reveal to babes these things that were hidden from the wise and prudent." And to His disciples He said," Blessed are you, for many prophets and kings have desired to see and hear what you have seen and H __ __ __ __." (Luke 10:21-24)

6 DOWN: A lawyer attempting to test Jesus asked what he should do to inherit eternal life. When told he should love God with every fiber of his being, and love his neighbor as himself, he asked "Who is my N __ __ __ __ __ __ __?" (Luke 10:25-29)

7 ACROSS: Jesus answered by telling of a man attacked by robbers and left for dead. Although a priest and a Levite passed that way, it was the S __ __ __ __ __ __ __ __ that stopped and took care of him. (Luke 10:30-35)

8 DOWN: When Jesus then asked which of the three was neighbor to the man, the lawyer responded, "He who showed M __ __ __ __." Then Jesus said to him, "Go and do likewise." (Luke 10:36-37)

9 DOWN: It happened that at a certain village on their way, they were welcomed into Martha and Mary's H __ __ __ __. Mary sat by Jesus attentive to all he was teaching, but Martha was distracted with serving her guests. (Luke 10:38-40)

10 ACROSS: She appealed to Jesus to tell Mary to help her, but Jesus answered "Martha, you are concerned about many things, but one thing is needed and Mary has C __ __ __ __ __ that good part, which will not be taken away from her." (Luke 10:41-42)

(To be continued ...)

SEVENTY; PEACE; NEAR; REJOICE; HEARD;
NEIGHBOR; SAMARITAN; MERCY; HOUSE; CHOSEN

LUKE

Chapter 10

highlights from **LUKE … chapter 11**

1 DOWN: On one occasion, after Jesus had been P __ __ __ __ __ __ one of His disciples asked him to teach them how to pray so Jesus said, "When you pray say: Our Father in heaven, we hold your name holy. May your kingdom come and your will be done on earth as it is in heaven. Give us our daily bread and forgive us our sins, as we forgive those who are indebted to us. Lead us, not into temptation, but deliver us from the evil one." (Luke 11:1-4)

2 ACROSS: Jesus went on to say, "If you go to your friend at midnight to borrow bread, and he first responds 'don't bother me', he will eventually arise and give you all you need if you are P __ __ __ __ __ __ __ __ __." (Luke 11:5-8)

3 DOWN: "Everyone who asks receives; everyone who seeks, finds; and to him who knocks it will be opened. If you know how to give good gifts to your children, how much more will your H __ __ __ __ __ __ __ Father give the Holy Spirit to those who ask Him." (Luke 11:9-13)

4 DOWN: Some said of Jesus, "He casts out demons by Beelzebub, the ruler of demons"; and others wanted Him to show a sign from heaven. Jesus responded, "If Satan is divided against himself, how will his kingdom stand? When an unclean spirit leaves a man, and finding no resting place returns to find all clean but unoccupied, he will enter and dwell there with other spirits more W __ __ __ __ __ than himself." (Luke 11:24-26)

5 ACROSS: A woman in the crowd, raised her voice, blessing His mother, but Jesus said, "Those who H __ __ __ the word of God and keep it are more to be blessed." (Luke 11:27-28)

6 DOWN: To the crowds gathered Jesus went on to say, "An evil generation seeks a sign, and no sign will be given except the sign of Jonah the prophet. No one lights a lamp then hides it; take heed that the L __ __ __ __ that is in you is not really darkness." (Luke 11:29-32)

7 ACROSS: Jesus was dining at a Pharisee's house and they asked why he did not do the ceremonial washing before eating. The Lord replied, "You Pharisees make the outside clean, but your inward part is full of greed and wickedness. You tithe even of mint and herbs, but pass by justice and the L __ __ __ of God." (Luke 11:33-43)

8 ACROSS: "Woe to you lawyers, you give men unbearable burdens and offer no help; you show your approval of your fathers who killed the prophets, by building their tombs; you refuse to gain K __ __ __ __ __ __ __ __ and you prevent others from doing so." (Luke 11:44-52)

9 DOWN: As He spoke, the scribes and Pharisees tried to make him say something that they could use A __ __ __ __ __ __ him. (Luke 11:53)

(To be continued …)

PRAYING; PERSISTENT; HEAVENLY; WICKED;
HEAR; LIGHT; LOVE; KNOWLEDGE; AGAINST

LUKE

Chapter 11

F H C V I R N G J E D W K L O P
D V X Y D E Q R U Z A N A G R H
K E B C F N L I M P O J L E U N
D F N R S E T H Q C V T D U K V
S K A E W C O T K J W A N Z Q C
P F L A P B Y M E B D B G K P G
M B L I U O R W L X N W I S U B
U K I D F Z L U M H I X V A C J
D A W J S L B J H L F K E E S W
L S F N I T Q C L H P U N P G C
Y K L W H L L Q N V H O W A K E
E O D M T F U R J B M Y F V S I

Luke, chapter 11 verse 9

Ask and it will be given to you, seek, and
you will find, knock and it will be opened.

E G B U H Q M F I D C V J K N O
S U W X C D N A T Y B A Z F F G
M J C B E M K H L O K I N D T M
C P F Q R O S G N I H T S V J U
R J G M V D N C W I V Z M Y P B
O E I Y O G X L Y T C A F J A F
L A V H T N Q V H W L V H R P U
T J E C P I F E L F H W I L L O
C X N L W K S I G U A R V U F Y
K R O M H E P B V P J T D O F B
X J K V E I L A M U G N W Y J D
D N Y K T C S L I A L Q E U R H

Luke, chapter 12 verse 31

Seek His (God's) kingdom and these things
will be given to you as well.

highlights from **LUKE … chapter 12**

1 DOWN: Jesus addressing his disciples, before the crowd, said, "Beware the hypocrisy of the Pharisees for there is nothing covered that will not be revealed. Do not be afraid of those who kill the body. S __ __ __ __ __ __ __ are not forgotten by God, and you are of more value than many sparrows." (Luke 12:1-6)

2 ACROSS: "Also I say, he who denies me before men will be denied before the A __ __ __ __ __ of God. When they bring you before the magistrates do not worry, the Holy Spirit will teach you in that very hour what you ought to say." (Luke 12:7-12)

3 DOWN: Then one from the crowd said," Teacher, tell my brother to divide the inheritance with me." But Jesus said to him, "One's L __ __ __ does not consist in the abundance of possessions." Jesus then told a parable of a rich man who said to himself, 'Soul you have many goods to last many years, take ease, eat, drink and be merry.' (Luke 12:13-20)

4 ACROSS: "But God said to him, 'Fool! This night your S __ __ __ will be required of you; then whose will all those things be?' So is he who lays up treasure for himself but is not rich toward God." (Luke 11:24-26)

5 ACROSS: "Life is more than food and the body more than clothing. The W __ __ __ __ seeks after all these things, and your Father knows what you need. But seek the kingdom of God and all these things shall be added to you." (Luke 12:27-31)

6 DOWN: "Your Father is pleased to give you the kingdom. Where your T __ __ __ __ __ __ __ is, there your heart will also be." (Luke 12:32-34)

7 ACROSS: Jesus went on to tell a parable of a man who needed to be prepared because he knew not what hour a thief might break into his house. In like manner the Son of Man is coming at an hour you do not expect, so you also be R __ __ __ __. (Luke 12:35-43)

8 DOWN: Blessed is the servant who is faithful and wise during his master's absence; he will be rewarded. But the servant who, in his master's absence, beats his fellow servant and gets drunk, will be P __ __ __ __ __ __ __. (Luke 12:44-48)

9 DOWN: Jesus said that his coming brings divisions: father A __ __ __ __ __ __ son, mother against daughter, in-laws against each other. (Luke 12:49-53)

10 ACROSS: Jesus also said to the crowds, "You discern the weather from the appearance of the sky, how is it you do not D __ __ __ __ __ __ this present time. You even do not judge what is right for yourselves. I tell you, when you have an adversary, try hard to be reconciled before it reaches the magistrates." (Luke 12:54-59)

(To be continued …)

SPARROWS; ANGELS; LIFE; SOUL; WORLD;
TREASURE; READY; PUNISHED; AGAINST; DISCERN

LUKE

Chapter 12

highlights from **LUKE … chapter 13**

1 DOWN: Jesus was told of the Galileans whose blood was mixed with their sacrifices. He answered, "Do you think these Galileans were worse S __ __ __ __ __ __ than others? Unless you repent you too will all perish." (Luke 13:1-5)

2 ACROSS: He then told this parable, "A man had a fig tree that bore no fruit over three seasons. He ordered the man who took care of his vineyard to cut it down, but he replied, 'Sir, give it one more year; I'll dig around it and F __ __ __ __ __ __ __ __ it and if it still bears no fruit next year, then cut it down.'" (Luke 13:6-8)

3 DOWN: It was a Sabbath and Jesus was T __ __ __ __ __ __ __ in the synagogue. He called forward a woman who had been crippled by a spirit for eighteen years, and said "Woman, you are set free from your infirmity." Then he put his hands on her and immediately she straightened up and praised God. (Luke 13:9-13)

4 DOWN: The synagogue leader indignantly told the people that there are six days for work, "Come for healing on one of those days not on the Sabbath." The Lord answered by saying, "Don't you untie you're A __ __ __ __ __ __ on the Sabbath; then should not this woman be set free on the Sabbath?" (Luke 13:14-17)

5 DOWN: Jesus continued, "The kingdom of God is like a mustard S __ __ __ that grew into a tree and the birds perched in its branches. It is like yeast mixed into sixty pounds of flour until it worked through all the dough." (Luke 13:18-21)

6 ACROSS: Jesus journeyed toward Jerusalem, teaching in towns and villages on the way. Answering someone's question He said, "Strive to enter through the narrow D __ __ __. Many will be told, 'I do not know where you come from; depart from me all you workers of evil.' And behold some are last who will be first, and some are first who will be last." (Luke 13:22-30)

7 DOWN: At that very hour some P __ __ __ __ __ __ __ __ warned Jesus, "Get away from here, for Herod wants to kill you." He responded, "Tell that fox, today and tomorrow I cast out demons and perform cures and the third day I finish my course." (Luke 13:31-32)

8 ACROSS: "Nevertheless, I must continue on my way, for a prophet cannot perish away from Jerusalem. O Jerusalem that kills the prophets. I would have gathered your children as a hen G __ __ __ __ __ __ her brood and you were not willing." (Luke 13:33-34)

9 DOWN: "Behold you will not see me until you say, 'Blessed is he who comes in the N __ __ __ of the Lord.'" (Luke 13:35)

(To be continued …)

SINNERS; FERTILIZE; TEACHING; ANIMALS;
SEED; DOOR; PHARISEES; GATHERS; NAME

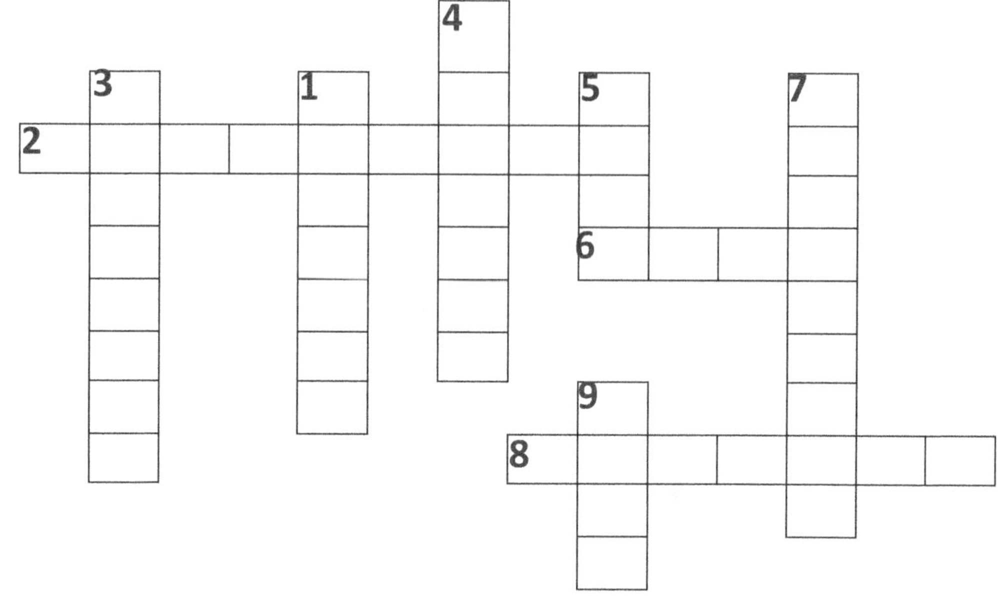

LUKE

Chapter 13

D	F	A	Q	G	P	L	E	H	C	B	U	I	J	M	N
R	T	V	W	B	C	X	D	O	O	R	E	T	N	E	F
M	I	F	A	D	L	J	G	K	N	J	H	H	C	S	L
F	W	B	P	P	C	R	S	O	C	T	N	R	U	I	T
Q	I	S	L	U	A	M	R	E	H	W	A	O	X	O	P
N	L	E	X	N	Y	C	K	Y	E	B	Z	U	T	A	Y
K	L	U	G	S	D	W	T	J	L	K	E	G	D	N	Z
S	I	N	B	M	X	E	O	E	Z	G	V	H	A	D	H
B	W	U	H	Q	J	R	H	R	T	Z	Q	M	T	E	V
J	Q	D	L	G	X	O	A	U	R	I	S	C	N	Y	A
W	I	J	U	F	P	I	Q	L	T	A	M	V	X	I	V
C	M	X	K	R	B	R	O	H	Z	K	N	D	T	P	G

Luke, chapter 13 verse 24

Strive to enter through the narrow door, for many, I tell you will seek to enter and will not be able.

A D F R E S M O E I S T I U R F
C I H M T W T F L M T R A P M I
R S E O R O Y T A E R U C N I S
E D N F N A M I P Z V O B A F H
M O S N E W V A T S E T W S T E
T M A L L C H S R F L I P D O C
P C B A U E O G A C P V A I X N
G E N G L D B S J L I E Y S A U
P K I X I N A S M H C F D G J O
B W F A N Y O N E G S P R C Y N
C N L W H S H Q N O I H W H K E
X O G M T P W R J B D F T V S R

Luke, chapter 14 verse 33

So therefore, anyone of you who does not renounce all that he has cannot be my disciple.

highlights from **LUKE … chapter 14**

1 DOWN: Jesus responded to the lawyers who watched Him as He dined at the H ___ ___ ___ ___ of the ruler of the Pharisees asking, "Is it lawful or not to heal on the Sabbath?" They had no answer. Then Jesus healed a man who had dropsy. (Luke 14:1-4)

2 ACROSS: And He said, "Which of you, having a son or an ox that has fallen into a well on the Sabbath, will not I ___ ___ ___ ___ ___ ___ ___ ___ ___ ___ pull him out?" And they could not reply. (Luke 14:5-6)

3 DOWN: Noticing how guests chose their seats He said to them, "Everyone who exalts himself will be H ___ ___ ___ ___ ___ ___ and he who humbles himself will be exalted." (Luke 14:7-11)

4 DOWN: And to His host He said "When you give a feast I ___ ___ ___ ___ ___ those who cannot invite you back or repay you and you will be blessed. For you will be repaid at the resurrection of the just." (Luke 14:12-14)

5 ACROSS: One of the guests hearing this said to Jesus, "Blessed is everyone who will eat bread in the K ___ ___ ___ ___ ___ ___ of God." (Luke 14:15)

6 DOWN: But Jesus responded by telling him of a man who gave a B ___ ___ ___ ___ ___ ___ and invited many. But when it was time for them to come to the banquet, they all made excuses. (Luke 14:16-17)

7 ACROSS: So, the man sent his servant to go into the streets and lanes and bring in the poor and the disabled; and when there were not enough to fill the banquet hall, he sent his servant out to the highways and hedges and compel people to come and F ___ ___ ___ the house. (Luke 14:17-24)

8 DOWN: Great crowds accompanied Jesus and he turned and said to them, "If anyone does not H ___ ___ ___ his own father and mother, wife and children, brothers and sisters, even his own life, he cannot be my disciple." (Luke 14:26-26)

9 ACROSS: "Whoever does not B ___ ___ ___ his own cross and come after me cannot be my disciple." (Luke 14:27)

10 ACROSS: "Who desiring to build a tower, does not first C ___ ___ ___ ___ the cost, otherwise he will be mocked when he has laid the foundation and is not able to finish." (Luke 14:28-32)

11 DOWN: "So therefore, anyone of you who does not renounce A ___ ___ he has cannot be my disciple." (Luke 14:33)

12 ACROSS: "S ___ ___ ___ that has lost its saltiness is of no use. It is thrown away. He who has ears to hear, let him hear." (Luke 14:34-35)

(To be continued …)

HOUSE; IMMEDIATELY; HUMBLED; INVITE; KINGDOM;
BANQUET; FILL; HATE; BEAR; COUNT; ALL; SALT

LUKE

Chapter 14

highlights from **LUKE … chapter 15 to 16**

1 DOWN: When the Pharisees and scribes saw tax collectors and sinners with Jesus they grumbled. He then told of a lost sheep that when found caused great rejoicing; and of a woman, who lost one of her ten silver coins and after diligently searching found it and called her friends to R __ __ __ __ __ __ with her. Just so, there is joy before the angels of God when one sinner repents. (Luke 15:1-10)

2 ACROSS: Then, Jesus told of the younger of a man's two sons who asked of his father to be immediately given his inheritance. The father complied, and the son took all that he had and went off to a far C __ __ __ __ __ __ where he squandered his property in reckless living. (Luke 15:11-13)

3 ACROSS: A famine then arose and he having nothing left, found himself working feeding pigs. He was so hungry that he decided to return to his father's house and offer himself as a hired S __ __ __ __ __ __. (Luke 15:14-19)

3 DOWN: The father, seeing his son coming in the distance ran to meet him, and embraced him. The son began to speak, "Father, I have S __ __ __ __ __, I am no longer worthy to be called your son." But the father instead ordered a celebration for his return. (Luke 15:20-28)

4 DOWN: The older S __ __ had been in the field, and as he approached the house, he heard the singing and dancing and asked what was happening. He became angry when he learned that his father was celebrating his brother's return. (Luke 15:20-28)

5 DOWN: "I have served you these many years and never have you given me a celebration". But his father replied, "All that is mine is yours; but this your brother was lost and now he is F __ __ __ __." (Luke 15:29-32)

6 ACROSS: Jesus said to his disciples, "A manager realizing he was about to be fired summoned his master's debtors and reduced each one's debt. The master, commended the manager for his shrewdness. If then you have not been F __ __ __ __ __ __ __ in the unrighteous wealth, who will entrust you the true riches?" (Luke 16:1-11)

7 DOWN: "No servant can serve two masters, for either he will hate the one and love the other. You cannot serve God and M __ __ __ __." Jesus knowing the Pharisees were ridiculing him because of their love of money, said to them, "What is exalted among men is an abomination in the sight of God." (Luke 16:12-17)

8 ACROSS: Jesus told of a P __ __ __ man, named Lazarus and a rich man who both died. The poor man went to paradise, the rich man to hades. The rich man being tormented in hades, asked that someone be sent to warn his brothers who were still alive. (Luke 16:18-29)

9 DOWN: But Abraham replied, "If they do not hear Moses and the prophets neither will they be convinced if someone should R __ __ __ from the dead. "(Luke 16:30)

(To be continued …)

REJOICE; COUNTRY; SERVANT; SINNED; SON;
FOUND; FAITHFUL; MONEY; POOR; RISE

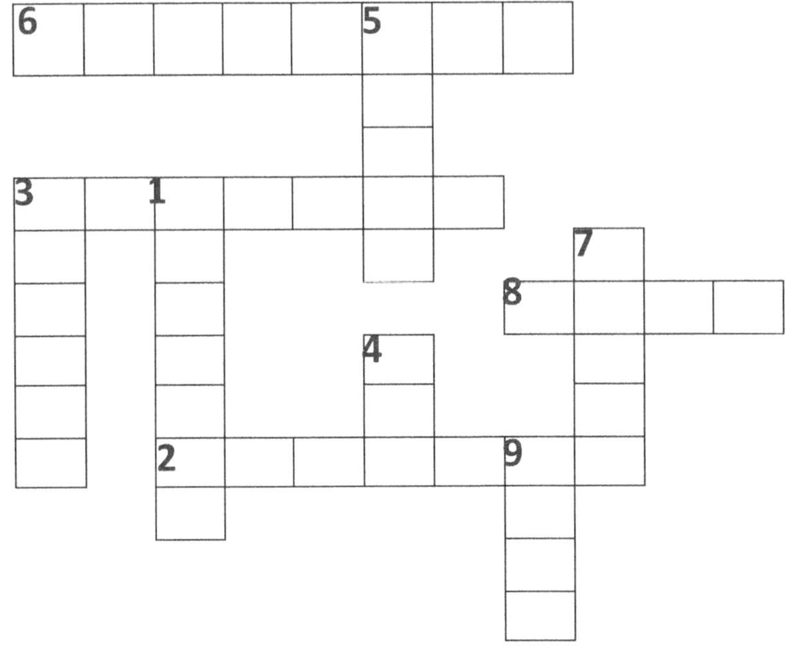

LUKE

Chapter 15 and 16

F N I R A G M T O I S D I U R G

I A H M T E C N H M U C H P M S

T O I A L V L N U E R A D N W P

E W R T F H J E A C I Q R T A K

V B T A H W T Y F H V J S U L E

R I L C I F G S B R N E M L O C

L D N T B P U C A M N Y A X S A

S E C T H E D L P O R H P E L R

P L S O G N M L H C U M K D A G

B W F K I H V S I G A L S O R S

N Y J U F P I E L T T I L N I W

C M X K R D R O H Z K P D T P G

Luke, chapter 16 verse 10

One who is faithful in a very little is also faithful in much, and one who is dishonest in a very little is also dishonest in much.

E G B U H Q M F I D C V J K N O
S U W X C D P P T Y B A Z F I G
M J G E B R O T H E R I N D T M
C P C Q W E U G P D U E S V J U
R J T M V B N O W I M Z P Y P B
O E I Y O U X L Y E V I G R O F
L H V H T K Q V K W L B H R N A
T J O C N E F T L F H W E Z B T
C X V S N I S Z G U A R V U F W
K R E M H Y P B S T N E P E R B
X J K V G R J P M U G N W Y J D
D N Y L S C T P I A L Q E U R H

Luke, chapter 17 verse 3

If your brother sins, rebuke him, and if he repents, forgive him …

highlights from **LUKE … chapter 17 to 18**

1 DOWN: Jesus said to his disciples, "Temptations are sure to come but woe to the one who brings them. Forgive your brother if he sins seven times and R ___ ___ ___ ___ ___ ___ each time." When you obey all you are commanded say, "I have only done my duty." (Luke 17:1-10)

2 ACROSS: On the way to Jerusalem, ten L ___ ___ ___ ___ ___ asked Jesus to have mercy on them. Jesus told them to go and show themselves to the priest (in accordance with Moses' law) and as they left, they found themselves healed. (Luke 17:11-14)

3 ACROSS: One of them, a Samaritan, returned to Jesus, praising God and giving thanks. Jesus asked him, "Where are the other N ___ ___ ___? Has only this foreigner returned to praise God? Rise and go your way; your faith has made you well." (Luke 17:15-19)

4 ACROSS: The Pharisees asked when the kingdom of God would come. Jesus answered, "the kingdom of God is in the M ___ ___ ___ ___of you." "Just as lightning can be seen from one side of the sky to the other, so will the Son of Man be in His day." (Luke 17:20-21)

5 ACROSS: "First He must be rejected by this generation. And just as in Noah's day before he entered the ark, and in Lot's day before Sodom was destroyed, so people will be eating and D ___ ___ ___ ___ ___ ___ ___, buying and selling, planting and building, when the Son of Man is revealed. (Luke 17:22-37)

6 DOWN: Jesus told a parable of a widow who was persistent in bringing her request for justice before a disrespectful J ___ ___ ___ ___. "Will not God give justice to his elect, who cry out to him day and night? Always pray and do not lose heart." (Luke 18:1-8)

7 DOWN: He also told a parable about the prayers of a Pharisee and a tax collector, saying everyone who E ___ ___ ___ ___ ___ himself will be humbled, but the one who humbles himself will be exalted. (Luke 18:9-14)

8 ACROSS: When the disciples rebuked those who brought children to Jesus, He said, "Whoever does not receive the kingdom of God L ___ ___ ___ a child shall not enter." (Luke 18:15-17)

9 DOWN: A R ___ ___ ___ ruler asked how to inherit eternal life. He became very sad when Jesus told him to sell all and follow him. "How difficult it is for the wealthy to enter the kingdom of God, but what is impossible with man is possible with God." (Luke 18:18-30)

10 DOWN: Jesus took the twelve aside and told them the prophesies will be accomplished: He would be delivered to the Gentiles, mocked, flogged and killed; and he would R ___ ___ ___ on the third day. But they did not grasp what He was saying. (Luke 18:31-34)

11 ACROSS: Near Jericho, Jesus healed a blind man who called out to him. "Recover your sight; your F ___ ___ ___ ___ has made you well." And all the people praised God. (Luke 18:35-43)

(To be continued …)

REPENTS; LEPERS; NINE; MIDST; DRINKING;
JUDGE; EXALTS; LIKE; RICH; RISE; FAITH

LUKE

Chapter 17 to 18

highlights from **LUKE … chapter 19**

1 DOWN: Zacchaeus, a rich tax collector, was a small man, so he climbed a sycamore tree in order to see Jesus, who at the time was passing through Jericho. Jesus saw him in the tree and said, "Hurry and come down, for T __ __ __ __ I must stay at your house." (Luke 19:1-5)

2 ACROSS: The people grumbled when they saw Jesus at Zacchaeus house. But Zacchaeus stood and said to Jesus "I will give half my goods to the poor, and to those I may have defrauded I will restore fourfold." Jesus responded, "Today S __ __ __ __ __ __ __ __ __ has come to this house. The Son of Man came to seek and save the lost." (Luke 19:6-10)

3 DOWN: Many near Jerusalem supposed that the kingdom of God was to appear immediately, so Jesus told this parable: A nobleman, before going away, gave $1000 to each of his ten servants telling them to 'do business 'till his R __ __ __ __ __. (Luke 19:11-14)

4 DOWN: On his return the first reported that he had made $1000 more. So, the nobleman commended him, "Well done, you have been F __ __ __ __ __ __ __ __ in little, I will put you in charge of ten of my businesses." The second made $500 more, and he too was commended and put in charge of five businesses. (Luke 19:15-19)

5 ACROSS: But another said, "Lord, you are known to be a severe man, so here is your money; I kept it wrapped up in a handkerchief." The nobleman took the money from him and gave it to the man who made $1000 more, saying, "Since I'm known to be severe, why didn't you put my money in the bank where it would earn interest." To everyone who has, more will be given., but from the one who has not, even what he has will be taken A __ __ __. (Luke 19:20-27)

6 ACROSS: Jesus continued on towards Jerusalem. He sent two of his disciples into the nearby village to retrieve a C __ __ __. Jesus rode it into Jerusalem. They spread their cloaks on it and along the road and the multitude began to rejoice and praise God saying, "Blessed is the king who comes in the name of the Lord!" (Luke 19:28-38)

7 ACROSS: Jesus responding to the Pharisees rebuke of this said, "If these were S __ __ __ __ __, the very stones would cry out." (Luke 19:39-40)

7 DOWN: As Jesus got closer to the city He wept saying, "The things that make for peace are hidden from your eyes. For, the days will come upon you when your enemies will tear you down to the ground, and not leave one S __ __ __ __ upon another because you did not know the time of your visitation." (Luke 19:41-44)

8 ACROSS: When Jesus entered the temple, He drove out those who were selling there saying, "It is written, 'My house shall be a house of P __ __ __ __ __', but you have made it into a den of robbers." (Luke 19:45-46)

9 DOWN: He taught D __ __ __ __ in the temple. The chief priests wanted to destroy him, but they could not because the people were hanging onto all His words. (Luke 19:47-48)

(To be continued …)

TODAY; SALVATION; RETURN; FAITHFUL;
AWAY; COLT; SILENT; STONE; PRAYER; DAILY

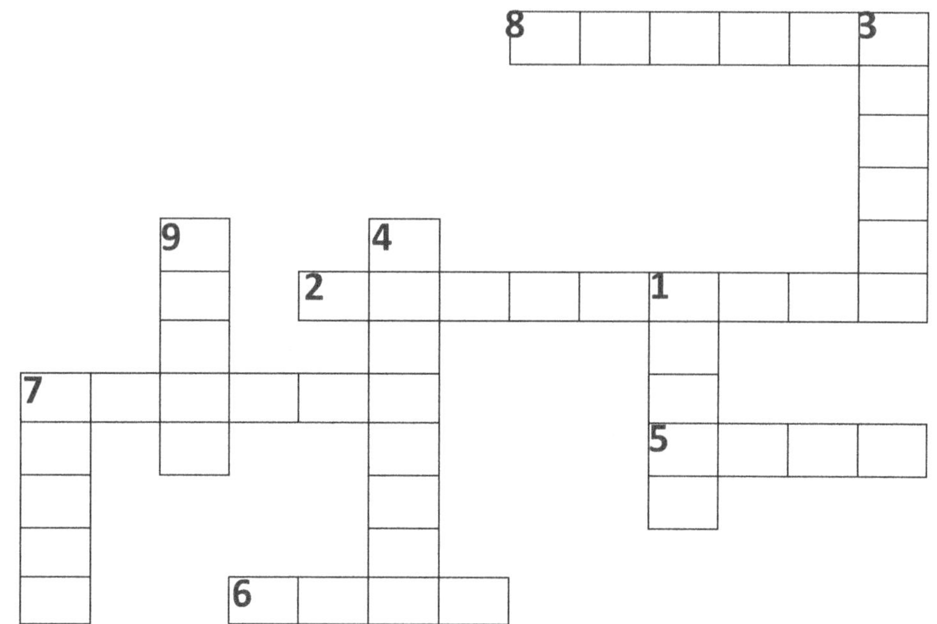

LUKE

Chapter 19

D	C	A	Q	G	P	L	E	H	C	B	U	I	J	M	N
R	T	V	W	B	C	N	O	S	X	A	Z	E	Y	E	F
M	R	F	A	D	L	J	G	K	N	J	H	M	C	S	L
G	P	B	H	P	C	R	F	O	C	T	Q	R	U	I	T
Q	I	S	E	N	A	M	R	V	H	W	Y	L	X	B	A
N	D	V	X	U	Y	W	K	E	Z	B	Z	A	I	N	Y
K	A	U	G	S	D	P	W	J	V	K	W	N	Q	G	Z
S	I	N	B	M	X	E	Z	K	E	G	T	D	Y	A	H
B	E	U	H	Q	J	R	H	X	C	S	Q	U	T	E	V
J	Q	E	L	G	X	O	A	U	O	A	S	C	N	Y	A
W	I	J	K	F	P	I	Q	L	T	F	M	V	X	I	V
C	M	X	U	R	B	R	O	H	Z	K	P	E	T	P	G

Luke, chapter 19 verse 10

For the Son of Man came to seek and to save the lost.

E	G	B	U	H	Q	M	F	I	D	C	V	J	K	E	O
S	U	W	X	C	D	P	P	T	Y	B	A	Z	N	F	G
M	T	G	B	S	M	K	H	L	O	K	I	O	D	T	M
C	P	O	Q	R	D	E	G	P	D	U	T	D	V	J	U
R	J	T	N	V	B	N	M	W	I	S	E	M	Y	P	B
O	G	F	Y	E	Z	X	L	O	R	T	A	T	J	O	F
L	A	E	H	T	O	Q	V	E	C	L	V	H	R	P	A
T	J	O	C	N	Y	F	N	E	F	E	W	E	Z	B	I
C	X	V	I	R	K	R	J	G	U	A	B	V	U	F	W
K	R	E	M	H	O	E	B	S	R	E	D	L	I	U	B
X	J	K	V	C	R	J	P	M	U	G	N	W	Y	J	D
D	N	Y	L	S	C	T	P	I	A	L	Q	E	U	R	H

Luke, chapter 20 verse 17

The stone that the builders rejected has become the cornerstone.

highlights from LUKE ... chapter 20

1 DOWN: As Jesus was T __ __ __ __ __ __ __ and preaching in the temple, the chief priests, scribes, and elders challenged Him, asking who gave Him authority to do these things. Jesus answered them by asking, if the baptism of John was from heaven or from man. (Luke 20:1-4)

2 ACROSS: Knowing that if they said it was from heaven, Jesus would ask why then did they not B __ __ __ __ __ __; and if they said from man, then the crowd would stone them, they answered that they did not know. And Jesus said, "Neither will I tell you by what authority I do these things." (Luke 20:5-8)

3 ACROSS: Then He began a parable: A man before going away, planted a vineyard and let it out to tenants. At harvest time he sent a servant to collect his portion but the tenants beat the servant and sent him away E __ __ __ __-handed. (Luke 20:9-10)

4 DOWN: He sent a second who they also B __ __ __ and sent away empty handed. Then he sent a third servant, who they wounded and also sent away empty handed. (Luke 20:11-12

5 DOWN: Finally, the man sent his son; but thinking that they could inherit the vineyard, they killed the son. Jesus added surely the owner of the vineyard will come and destroy those tenants and give the vineyard to O __ __ __ __ __. (Luke 20:13-15)

6 ACROSS: The scribes and chief priests realizing the parable was about them, set about trying to trick him at every opportunity. Jesus knowing their craftiness answered their question about the lawfulness of paying taxes to Caesar, by pointing to the image on a coin and saying, "R__ __ __ __ __ to Caesar the things that are Caesar's, and to God the things that are God's." (Luke 20:16-27)

7 DOWN: The Sadducees, who deny the R __ __ __ __ __ __ __ __ __ __ __, asked Jesus about a woman who had been married and been widow to seven brothers. "Whose wife will she be in the resurrection?" Jesus answered, "In the resurrection they do not marry for they cannot die; God is not God of the dead but of the living." (Luke 20:28-40)

8 ACROSS: But Jesus put this question to them, "How can they say that the Christ is David's son when David calls him L __ __ __ in the Psalm: 'The Lord said to my Lord, sit at my right hand until I make your enemies your footstool.'" (Luke 20:41-44)

9 ACROSS: And in the hearing of all the people He said to His disciples, "Beware of the scribes who walk around in long robes, take the B __ __ __ seats in places of honor, devour widow's houses, and for a pretense make long prayers. They will receive the greater condemnation." (Luke 20:45-47)

(To be continued ...)

TEACHING; BELIEVE; EMPTY; BEAT; OTHERS;
RENDER; RESURRECTION; LORD; BEST

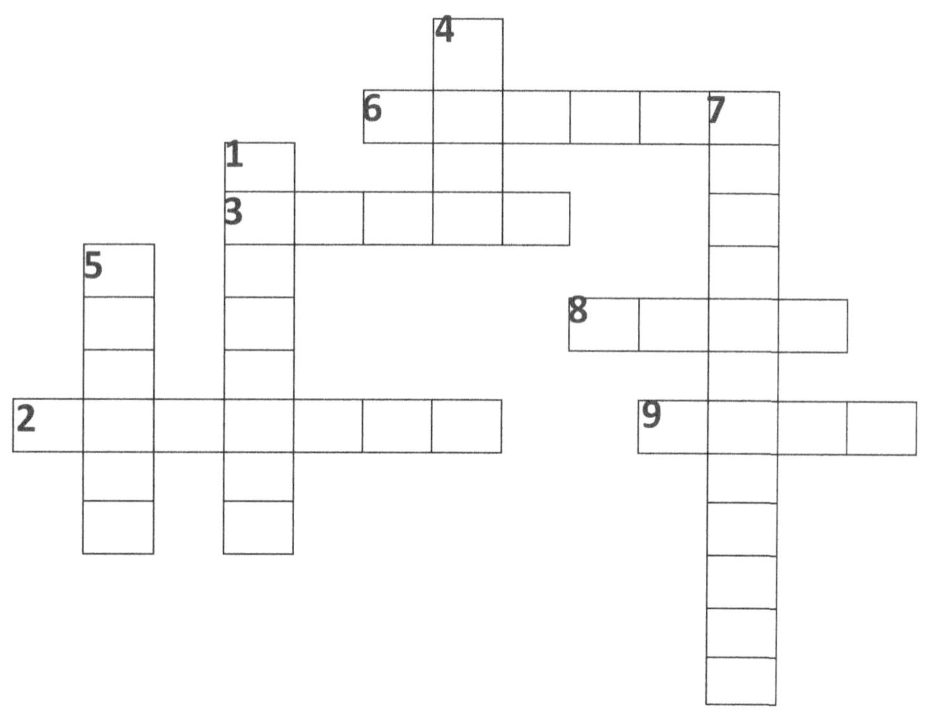

LUKE

Chapter 20

highlights from **LUKE … chapter 21**

1 DOWN: Jesus noticed rich people putting their gifts in the offering box and a poor widow put two small copper coins in the box. And He said, "This widow has put more in than all of them because she, out of her P _ _ _ _ _ _ put in her all." (Luke 21:1-4)

2 ACROSS: As some people spoke admiring the adornments of the T _ _ _ _ _, Jesus said, "The days will come when there will not be left here, one stone that will not be thrown down." (Luke 21:5-6)

3 ACROSS: They asked him "How will we know when this is about to happen?" and He answered, "Don't be led astray by the many saying, 'the T _ _ _ is at hand', Don't be terrified by the news of wars, earthquakes, famines and epidemics. These things must first occur but the end will not be immediate." (Luke 21:7-9)

4 ACROSS: "But before all this you will be persecuted and I _ _ _ _ _ _ _ _ _ and brought before kings and governors for my sake. Don't fret about what to say, I will give you words of wisdom that no adversary will be able to contradict." (Luke 21:10-15)

5 DOWN: "You will be turned in by parents, siblings, relatives and F _ _ _ _ _ _; some of you will even be put to death. You will be hated because of me, but you will not perish for by your endurance you will gain your lives." (Luke 21:16-19)

6 DOWN: "When you see Jerusalem surrounded by armies its desolation is near. Then if in Judea, flee to the mountains; if in the city, get out; if you are in the C _ _ _ _ _ _ don't come into the city. Jerusalem will be trampled underfoot by Gentiles until the fulfillment of the Gentiles' times." (Luke 21:20-24)

7 DOWN: "There will be S _ _ _ _ in the natural world. And then the Son of Man will be seen coming in a cloud with power and great glory. When these things begin, pay attention, your redemption is drawing near." (Luke 21:25-28)

8 DOWN: Then He told a parable: As with the fig tree and the other trees, when L _ _ _ _ _ begin to bud you know summer is already near; so, when you see these things, you know the kingdom of God is near. (Luke 21:29-33)

9 ACROSS: "Don't be caught off guard by the pleasures and cares of life, for that day may come upon you S _ _ _ _ _ _ _ like a trap. Pray that you may stand before the Son of Man and have strength to escape the things that are going to take place." (Luke 21:34-36)

10 ACROSS: Early each morning the people came to the temple to H _ _ _ Jesus. He lodged at night on Mount Olive and returned to teach every day. (Luke 21:37-38)

(To be continued …)

POVERTY; TEMPLE; TIME; IMPRISONED; FRIENDS;
COUNTRY; SIGNS; LEAVES; SUDDENLY; HEAR

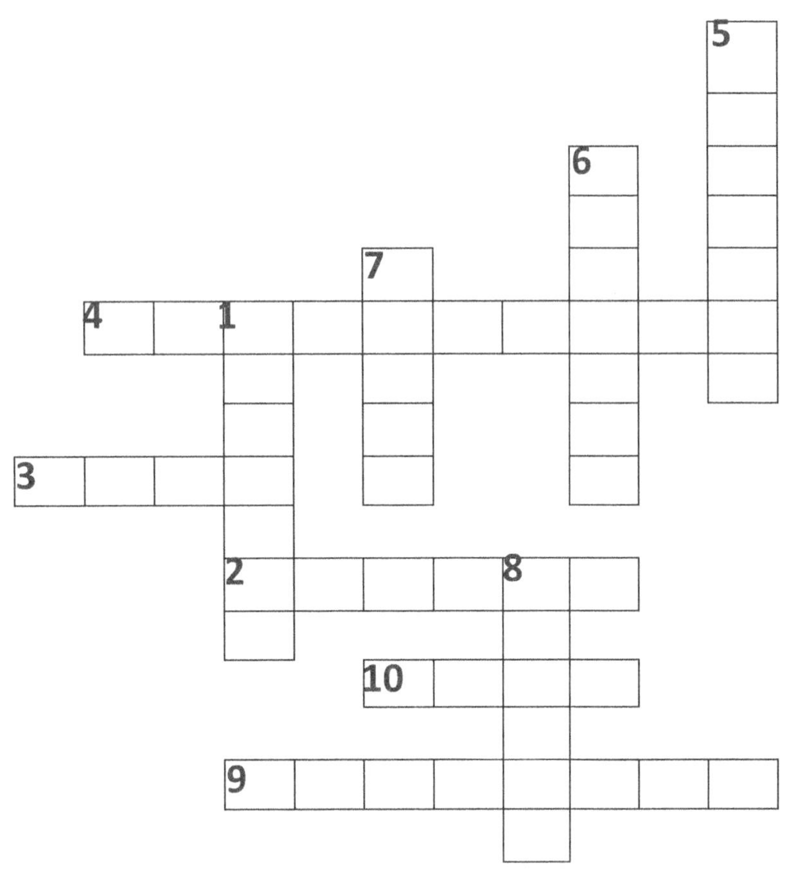

LUKE

Chapter 21

F H C V I R N G J E D W K L O P
T V X Y D E Q R U Z A B A G R H
N K H C F N L I M P L J O E U N
G S D R O W T H Y E V Q T U B V
S K U T E C O T X J W A N Z Q C
P S S A P B D M W B D B G K P G
R B W I U F R I L X M W H S U B
U O P D O Z L U M H I T F A C J
D F W Y S L T J H V R S W V G W
L S F A I T Q C W A K U E P G C
Y K L W H E A V E N H O W A K E
E O D A T F U R J D M R F V S I

Luke, chapter 21 verse 33

Heaven and earth will pass away, but my (Jesus') words will not pass away.

F	N	I	T	A	E	M	T	O	I	S	D	I	U	L	G
I	Y	R	M	T	G	C	N	H	M	T	F	B	E	M	S
T	E	D	A	L	O	L	D	U	E	R	G	A	N	W	P
O	W	N	E	F	H	J	E	A	C	I	D	R	O	I	K
V	B	F	A	I	W	G	Y	T	H	E	J	V	F	L	T
R	Q	L	T	S	E	T	A	E	R	G	S	P	L	S	C
E	D	A	F	B	P	K	C	A	M	H	Y	A	E	N	A
S	E	V	R	E	S	D	X	P	I	F	H	G	I	W	N
P	L	S	O	G	N	M	L	F	H	S	N	K	D	O	D
B	W	F	K	T	H	E	D	I	G	U	P	R	C	R	S
N	I	J	U	F	P	I	Q	L	O	F	M	V	X	I	W
C	M	X	K	R	B	R	T	Y	Z	K	P	D	T	P	G

Luke, chapter 22 verse 26

Let the greatest among you be as the youngest, and the leader as one who serves.

highlights from **LUKE … chapter 22**

1 DOWN: As the P __ __ __ __ __ __ __ feast approached the scribes and chief priests plotted how to put Jesus to death, but were afraid of the crowds. Then Satan entered Judas Iscariot and he went to them and schemed how to betray Jesus when He was away from the crowds. And they gladly agreed to give him money. (Luke 22:1-6)

2 ACROSS: On the day of the sacrifice, Jesus sent Peter and John to make preparations. They found a large furnished upper R __ __ __, just as Jesus had described it. At mealtime Jesus said to the apostles, "I have earnestly desired to eat this with you before I suffer, for I will not eat it until it is fulfilled in the kingdom of God." (Luke 22:6-16)

3 ACROSS: When He had given thanks, He broke bread and said, "This is my B __ __ __ which is given for you; do this in remembrance of me." And after they had eaten, he took the cup of the fruit of the vine and said, "This cup that is poured out for you is the new covenant in my blood." (Luke 21:10-15)

4 DOWN: "Behold my betrayer's hand is on the table; the Son of Man goes as it has been determined, but woe to that M __ __ by whom He is betrayed." And the apostles questioned amongst themselves which of them was the betrayer. (Luke 22:16-23)

5 ACROSS: They disputed amongst themselves as to which was the G __ __ __ __ __ __ __. Jesus said "Let the greatest and the leader among you become as one who serves. I am among you as the one who serves." (Luke 22:24-30)

6 DOWN: Then Peter said, "Lord I am willing to go with you to both prison and death." "And Jesus said "Peter, the rooster will not crow this day until you deny T __ __ __ __ times, that you know me." (Luke 22:31-34)

7 ACROSS: As was Jesus' custom He and the disciples went to the mount of Olives. Jesus withdrew about a stone's throw from them and He earnestly P __ __ __ __ __, "Father, if you are willing, remove this cup from me. Nevertheless, not my will but yours." (Luke 22:35-46)

8 DOWN: When he arose from prayer and was speaking to the disciples a crowd with swords and clubs, led by Judas approached and Judas kissed Him. Then they seized Him and brought him to the high priest's house. P __ __ __ __ followed at a distance. (Luke 22:47-54)

9 ACROSS: Peter denied knowing Jesus to a servant girl who thought she recognized him as a disciple, and a little after that to a man who also thought he recognized him, and about an hour after that to a man who insisted he recognized him; then a rooster crowed and Peter went out and W __ __ __ bitterly. (Luke 22:55-62)

10 ACROSS: Those holding Jesus in custody beat and mocked Him. At daybreak they took Him to their council and they all said, "If you are the Christ tell us. Are you the S __ __ of God?" Jesus replied, "You say that I am." And they said, "What further testimony do we need?" (Luke 22:63-71)

(To be continued …)

PASSOVER; ROOM; BODY; MAN; GREATEST;
THREE; PRAYED; PETER; WEPT; SON

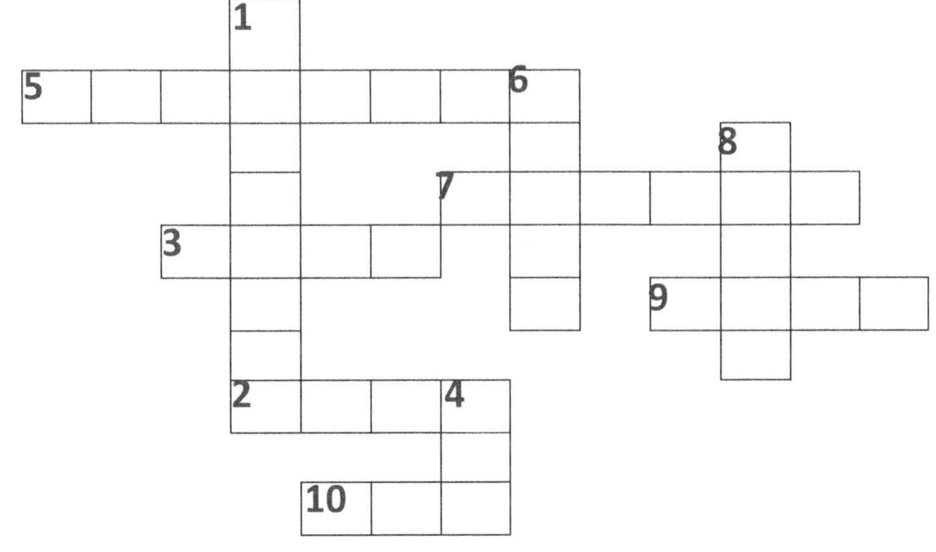

LUKE

Chapter 22

highlights from LUKE … chapter 23

1 DOWN: Jesus was brought before P __ __ __ __ __ and accused of forbidding the paying of taxes and saying that He was a king. Pilate asked Him if He was king of the Jews and Jesus answered, "You have said so." Pilate, turning to the chief priests and the crowds said, "I find no fault in this man." (Luke 23:1-4)

2 ACROSS: But they insisted that He had stirred up the people with his teaching from Galilee to here. When Pilate learned Jesus was from Galilee, he passed Him on to H __ __ __ __, who was in charge of Galilee and was in Jerusalem at the time. (Luke 23:5-7)

3 ACROSS: Herod questioned Jesus at length. Herod and his soldiers mocked Him, dressed Him in splendid clothing and sent Him B __ __ __ to Pilate, who called back the chief priests saying that neither he nor Herod found Jesus guilty of any of the charges. (Luke 23:8-14)

4 DOWN: Pilate said, "He has done nothing deserving D __ __ __ __. I will punish and release him." But the crowds shouted "Release Barabbas instead!" Pilate appealed to them three times but they continued with their demands to crucify Jesus. (Luke 23:15-23)

5 ACROSS: So, Pilate gave in to their demands, releasing Barabbas, who was an insurrectionist, and delivering Jesus to be C __ __ __ __ __ __ __ __. They seized hold of Simon of Cyrene to carry the cross behind Jesus as they led Him away. (Luke 23:24-26)

6 DOWN: Jesus turned to the women in the crowd that was following them and said, "Do not weep for me but W __ __ __ for yourselves and your children; for if they do these things when the wood is green, what will happen when it is dry." (Luke 23:27-31)

7 DOWN: They crucified Jesus along with two criminals at a place that is called "The Skull". And Jesus said, "Father, F __ __ __ __ __ __ them for they know not what they do." They cast lots for His garments; people watched; rulers scoffed; soldiers mocked. The inscription over Him read, "This is the King of the Jews." (Luke 23:32-38)

8 ACROSS: One of the criminals crucified with Him railed at Him, but the other said," We are receiving what we deserve but He has done N __ __ __ __ __ __ wrong. Then he said to Jesus, "Remember me when you come into your kingdom." And Jesus said to him, "Today you will be with me in paradise." (Luke 23:39-43)

9 DOWN: From about 12 noon to 3pm there was no sunlight, and the C __ __ __ __ __ __ of the temple was torn in two. Then Jesus called out, "Father into your hands I commit my spirit." And He breathed His last. The centurion, seeing all this, praised God saying, "Surely this man was innocent." (Luke 23:44-49)

10 DOWN: Joseph of Arimathea, a member of the council who had not agreed to their actions, asked Pilate for Jesus' body. He wrapped it and placed it in a new T __ __ __ cut in the stone. The women who came with him, then went away to prepare spices and ointments before resting, as the Sabbath was beginning. (Luke 23:50-56)

(To be continued …)

PILATE; HEROD; BACK; DEATH; CRUCIFIED;
WEEP; FORGIVE; NOTHING; CURTAIN; TOMB

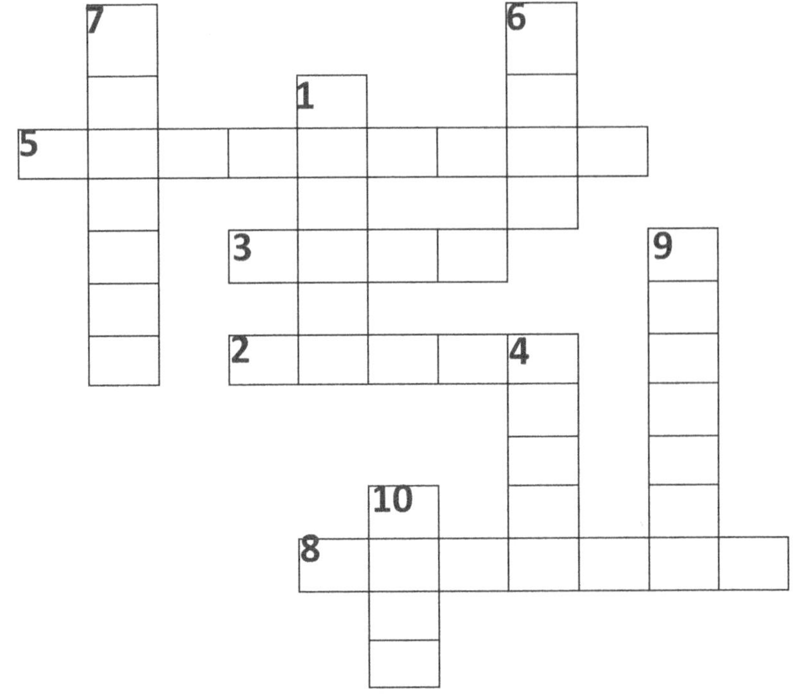

LUKE

Chapter 23

A D F R E S M O E I S T I U R F
C I B M T W T F L M T R A P M K
R S E O R E B T A E R E C J N S
D H R F I A V D P Z V O B O F H
T O S T E W C I T S P T W S T E
R M S C V L H S G E F I H D X C
P H B A U E F G A R L V A E N A
G E N G L D B S J L O E T S Y R
P K I X Y N R E H T A F D Z J G
B W F A E J V D A C N P R C E N
C N L W H S L Q N V H O W H A T
X O G M T P U R J B M F T V S B

Luke, chapter 23 verse 34

And Jesus said, "Father, forgive them, for they know not what they do.

A Z B Y H X D W E V F U D T H S
I R J Q K P R O G N S H A Z D W
B Y F U L O P L N Q G C G A R N
R E C V C V T H I E V T B U K V
K N U N D A E D V F W A N E Q C
P E J A P B Y M I B G B E K P G
M S W G N O M A L X M S I L U B
U I P Z F Z G U M H I X F A C J
G R W J P B E D O V K J Q V F P
L S F N E T Q C W E K U E P G C
B K L W H Y L Q N V H O W A K E
A O G M T P U R J B M T F V S B

Luke, chapter 24 verse 5b to 6a

Why do you seek the living among the dead. He is not here, He is risen.

highlights from LUKE ... chapter 24

1 DOWN: Very early on the day after the S __ __ __ __ __ __, the women went to Jesus' tomb but found His body was missing. They were perplexed. Then two men in dazzling apparel stood by them saying, "Why seek the living among the dead; He is risen." (Luke 24:1-7)

2 ACROSS: Then Mary Magdalene, Joanna, Mary (the mother of James), and the other women remembered what He had said and went off to tell the eleven apostles, and the other disciples. Not believing them, Peter ran to the tomb, saw it was E __ __ __ __ and the linen wrapping cloths were lying by themselves, and he marveled. (Luke 24:8-12)

3 ACROSS: That day Cleopas and another disciple, on their way to Emmaus, a village about seven miles from J __ __ __ __ __ __ __ __, were discussing all that had happened, when Jesus joined them. Not immediately recognizing Him, Cleopas said, "Are you just now visiting Jerusalem?", when Jesus inquired about their conversation. (Luke 24:13-18)

4 DOWN: They told Him about Jesus of Nazareth, the mighty prophet who they thought would redeem Israel; that T __ __ __ __ days ago He was crucified. They told Him of the women and others who had found the tomb empty. (Luke 24:19-24)

5 ACROSS: Then Jesus said to them, "O foolish ones, and slow to believe the words of the prophets who told it was necessary for C __ __ __ __ __ to suffer these things and enter glory." Then beginning with Moses, He explained the Scriptures to them. (Luke 24:24-26)

6 DOWN: It was L __ __ __ as they approached the village so they urged Him to stay with them as He seemed to have further to go. He stayed, and as they ate He blessed and broke the bread. They then recognized Him and He vanished from their sight. (Luke 24:27-31)

7 DOWN: They said to each other, "Weren't our H __ __ __ __ __ stirred as he explained the Scriptures to us?" They immediately returned to Jerusalem to tell the others, who in turn told them, "The Lord is risen indeed, and has appeared to Simon!" (Luke 24:32-35)

8 DOWN: As they were all talking Jesus appeared. He calmed their fears (for they thought He was a ghost} saying, "Do not doubt, touch me, a ghost does not have F __ __ __ __ and bones." They hesitated, so he asked for food and ate in their presence. (Luke 24:36-43)

9 ACROSS: Then reminding them of His words when He was with them, He explained the Scriptures that prophesied the Christ should suffer and on the third day rise from the D __ __ __; and that repentance for forgiveness of sins should be proclaimed to all nations, beginning at Jerusalem. (Luke 24:44-47)

10 ACROSS: "You are witnesses to these things; and I will send the promise of my Father upon you. But stay in the city until you are clothed with power from on high." Then leading them out of the city to Bethany, He lifted His H __ __ __ __ in a blessing and was carried up to heaven. They worshipped Him and returned to Jerusalem with joy and were continually in the temple blessing God. (Luke 24:48-51)

(To be continued ...)

SABBATH; EMPTY; JERUSALEM; THREE;
CHRIST; LATE; HEARTS; FLESH; DEAD; HANDS

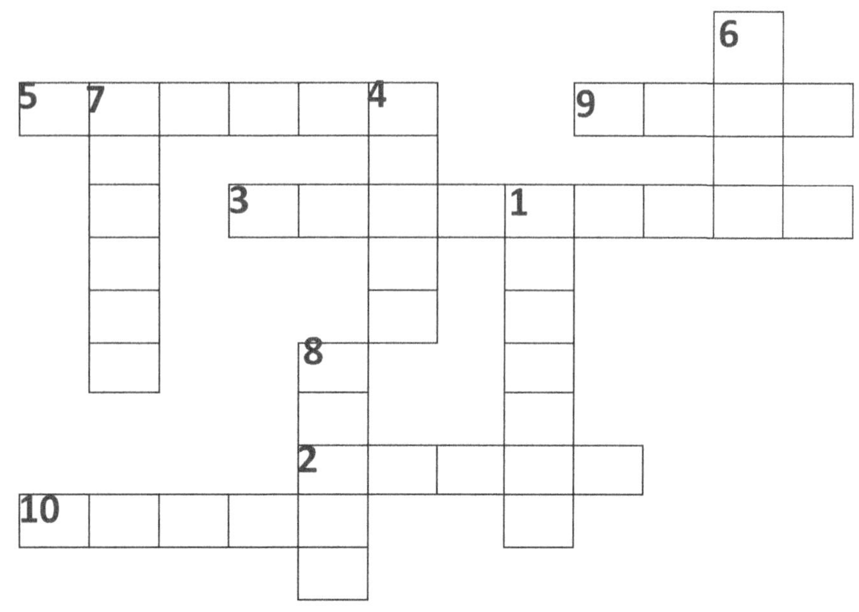

LUKE

Chapter 24

(Highlights from)

Of the Apostles

Chapter 1 verses 1 to 3

To: My most excellent Theophilus
From: Dr. Luke
Subject: A continuation of the earlier account of the things that Jesus did and taught.

highlights from **ACTS … chapter 1**

1 DOWN: O Theophilus, the first book dealt with all Jesus did and taught up until his ascension. He had appeared alive to the A ___ ___ ___ ___ ___ ___ ___, after his sufferings, speaking about the kingdom of God. (Acts 1:1-3)

2 ACROSS: He had ordered them to wait in J ___ ___ ___ ___ ___ ___ ___ ___ for the promise of the Father, "for John baptized with water, but you will be baptized with the Holy Spirit not many days from now." (Acts 1:4-5)

3 ACROSS: In response to their questioning if this was when He would restore the kingdom of Israel, He said, "It is not for you to know times the Father has fixed. But you will receive P ___ ___ ___ ___ when the Holy Spirit has come upon you, and you will be my witnesses in Jerusalem and beyond and to the end of the earth." (Acts 1:6-9))

4 ACROSS: As they watched Him speaking, He was lifted up, and a C ___ ___ ___ ___ took Him out of sight. As they gazed, two men in white robes stood beside them and said to them, "Men of Galilee, why do you stand looking heavenward? This Jesus who was taken up from you into heaven, will come in the same way as you saw Him go." (Acts 1:10-11)

5 DOWN: They returned to Jerusalem, a Sabbath day's journey from mount Olivet where they had been staying. All E ___ ___ ___ ___ ___ remaining apostles gathered in their upper room and together with the women, Jesus' mother and His brothers devoted themselves to prayer. (Acts 1:12-14)

6 ACROSS: P ___ ___ ___ ___ stood up in the company of about one hundred and twenty, and said, "Scripture was fulfilled concerning Judas, who was guide to those who arrested Jesus. He was numbered among us and was allotted his share in this ministry. (Acts 1:15-17)

7 DOWN: For it is written in the book of Psalms, "Let another take his office." So, one of the men who accompanied us all the time the Lord Jesus was amongst us, must become with us a W ___ ___ ___ ___ ___ ___ to His resurrection." (Acts 1:18-22)

8 ACROSS: And they put forward T ___ ___ names: Joseph (aka Barsabbas aka Justus), and Matthias. (Acts 1:23)

9 DOWN: And they prayed and said, "You, Lord, who know the H ___ ___ ___ ___ ___ of all, show which of these two, you have chosen for this ministry of apostleship from which Judas turned aside. (Acts 1:24-25)

10 ACROSS: And they cast lots for them, and the lot fell on M ___ ___ ___ ___ ___ ___ ___, and he was numbered with the eleven apostles. (Acts 1:26)

(To be continued …)

APOSTLES; JERUSALEM; POWER; CLOUD; ELEVEN;
PETER; WITNESS; TWO; HEARTS; MATTHIAS

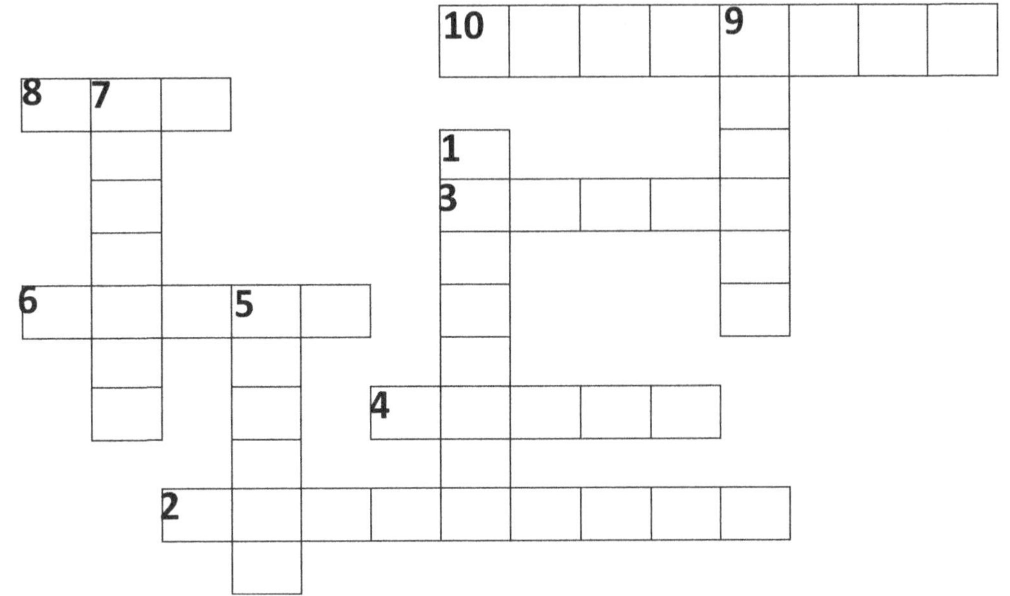

ACTS

Chapter 1

D	F	A	Q	G	P	L	E	H	B	T	U	I	J	M	N
R	T	V	W	B	N	O	D	X	S	E	M	O	C	E	B
M	I	F	A	D	L	O	G	U	N	J	H	G	F	S	L
F	D	E	I	N	A	P	M	O	C	C	A	R	U	I	T
Q	U	S	L	U	R	M	R	A	H	W	Y	L	X	O	A
N	I	K	W	N	Y	W	K	Y	Z	B	Z	K	I	N	Y
H	Z	U	G	A	H	P	W	I	T	N	E	S	S	G	Z
S	I	R	J	E	S	U	S	K	E	G	V	D	Y	A	H
B	W	U	N	Q	J	R	H	F	T	Z	Q	U	T	E	V
J	Q	N	O	I	T	C	E	R	R	U	S	E	R	Y	A
W	I	J	U	F	P	I	Q	L	T	F	M	V	X	I	V
C	M	X	K	R	B	R	O	H	W	K	P	D	T	P	G

Acts, chapter 1 verses 21-22

One who accompanied us when Jesus was among us … must become with us a witness to his resurrection.

B D L E H Q F M I G C V J K N R

Y U W X C D I H T A E D Z F O G

M J G B E H K B L S K I N D T M

C P C Q R D S G U D U R S V J U

R J T M V B N A W I V G M Y P B

O E F Y O Z C L Y A C N F J O F

L A V H T E Q V K W F I H R P A

T J G P B Y M T L O H S E Z B I

C X V D E S I A R U W O V U F W

K R E M C Y H B V A G O D T F B

X J K V G P O S S I B L E Y J D

D N Y L S C T H U A L Q W U R H

Acts, chapter 2 verse 24

God raised Him (Jesus) up loosing the pangs of death, because it was not possible for him to be held by it.

highlights from **ACTS ... chapter 2**

1 DOWN: On the day of Pentecost, a sudden sound, like a mighty rushing wind filled the house where the apostles had gathered. What appeared to be divided tongues of fire rested on each one, and filled with the Holy Spirit they spoke in other T __ __ __ __ __ __ as the Spirit gave them utterance. (Acts 2:1-4)

2 ACROSS: Devout Jews, from every nation were in J __ __ __ __ __ __ __ __, and they gathered, bewildered, amazed, and astonished at hearing the apostles speaking, each one hearing his own language. (Acts 2:5-11)

3 DOWN: All asked, "What does this mean?". But some M __ __ __ __ __ __ said. "They are filled with new wine." (Acts 2:12-13))

4 ACROSS: Peter, standing with the eleven addressed them, "These people are not D __ __ __ __. But this is fulfillment of what, through the prophet Joel, God declared, should be in the last days." (Acts 2:14-21)

5 ACROSS: He continued, "Men of Israel, hear these words: Jesus, at the foreknowledge of God, you crucified, but God R __ __ __ __ __ Him up. The patriarch David foresaw and spoke of the resurrection of Christ. And we all are witnesses of His resurrection. Therefore, know for certain that God has made Him both Lord and Christ, this Jesus, whom you crucified." (Acts 2:22-36)

6 ACROSS: Now when they heard this, they were cut to the heart and said to Peter and the rest of the apostles, "W __ __ __ must we do?" (Acts 2:37)

7 ACROSS: Peter said to them, "Repent and be B __ __ __ __ __ __ __, every one of you in the name of Jesus Christ for the forgiveness of your sins, and you will receive the gift of the Holy Spirit." (Acts 2:38-39)

8 DOWN: And with many other words he continued to exhort them. So those who received his word were baptized, and there were A __ __ __ __ that day about three thousand souls. (Acts 2:40-41)

9 ACROSS: They devoted themselves to the apostles' teaching, fellowship, the breaking of bread, and prayers. Many wonders and S __ __ __ __ were being done through the apostles. All who believed were together and had all things in common. (Acts 2:42-45)

10 ACROSS: And day by day, they were praising God and having favor with all people; and the Lord added to their number day by D __ __ those who were being saved. (Acts 2:46-47)

(To be continued ...)

TONGUES; JERUSALEM; MOCKING; DRUNK;
RAISED; WHAT; BAPTIZED; ADDED; SIGNS; DAY

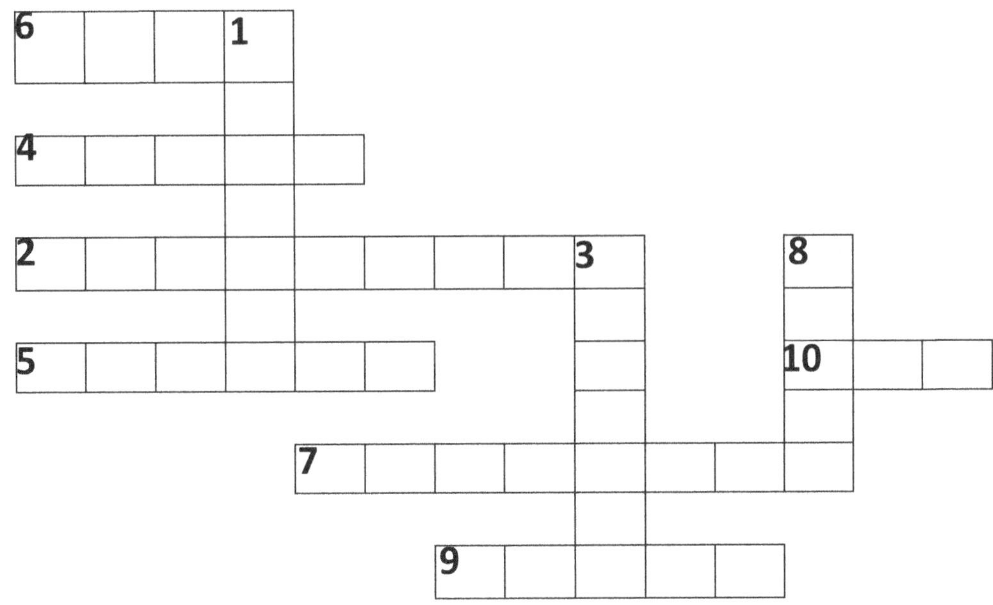

ACTS

Chapter 2

highlights from **ACTS … chapter 3**

1 DOWN: A man who each day was laid at the gate of the temple called the Beautiful Gate, was being carried there. On seeing Peter and John about to go into the temple, at the prayer hour, he B __ __ __ __ __ alms of them (Acts 3:1-3)

2 ACROSS: Peter looked directly at him, (as did John), and said, "Look at us." The man looked, expecting to receive something, but Peter said to him, "I have no silver and G __ __ __, but what I do have I give to you. In the name of Jesus Christ of Nazareth, rise up and walk!" And he took his right hand and raised him up, and immediately his feet and ankles were made strong. (Acts 3:4-7)

3 DOWN: He stood up leaping, and walked into the temple with them, L __ __ __ __ __ __ and praising God. The people in the temple recognized him and were filled with wonder and amazement. (Acts 3:8-10)

4 ACROSS: When P __ __ __ __ saw the people gathering at the part of the temple called Solomon's portico, he addressed them. "Men of Israel; why do you stare at us as if by our own power we made him walk." (Acts 3:11-12)

5 DOWN: "The God of Abraham, Isaac, and Jacob; the God of our fathers glorified his servant Jesus, when you asked Pilate to release a murderer instead of Him. You denied the Holy R __ __ __ __ __ __ __ __ One, and killed the Author of Life. But God raised Him from the dead; to this we are witnesses." (Acts 3:13-15)

6 ACROSS: "And faith, that is through J __ __ __ __, has made this man, who you see and know, strong and has given him perfect health in your presence." (Acts 3:16)

7 ACROSS: "Now brothers, I know that you and your rulers acted in ignorance. God fulfilled what He had foretold through the P __ __ __ __ __ __ __; that His Christ would suffer. Repent therefore so that your sins may be blotted out, and times of refreshing may come from the presence of the Lord; …" (Acts 3:17-19)

8 DOWN: "from Jesus, the appointed C __ __ __ __ __, whom heaven must receive until the time for restoring all the things God's holy prophets foretold long ago." (Acts 3:19-20)

9 ACROSS: "Moses said 'the L __ __ __ God will raise up a prophet like me and you shall listen to whatever He tells you; and those who do not listen will be destroyed. And all the prophets, from Samuel onward also proclaimed these days." (Acts 3:21-24)

10 DOWN: "You are the descendants of the prophets and of the C __ __ __ __ __ __ __ God made saying to Abraham, 'In your offspring shall all the families of the earth be blessed'. God having raised up His servant, sent Him to you first to bless you by turning every one of you from your wickedness." (Acts 3:25-26)

(To be continued …)

BEGGED; GOLD; LEAPING; PETER; RIGHTEOUS;
JESUS; PROPHETS; CHRIST; LORD; COVENANT

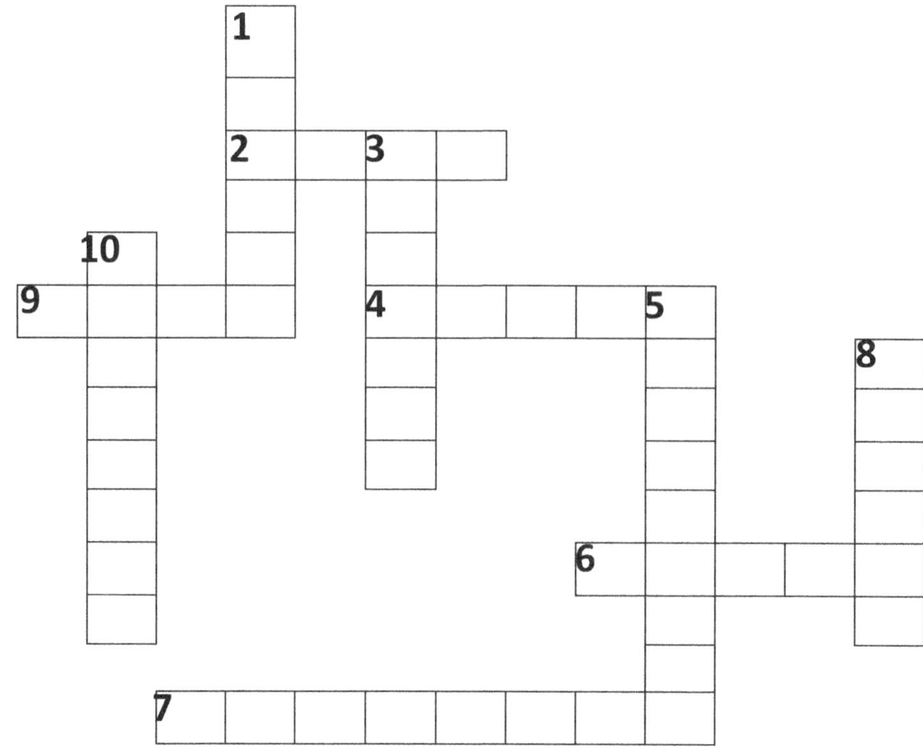

ACTS

Chapter 3

H N I R A E C T S I S D I U R G

I Y F M T X O G H E T F B P W S

T O D A L V F N U A I A D N I P

A U R E F H F I C R D L R U L K

V R F A S W S Y F H V J I T L E

B Q L C B E P A B R A H A M O C

J L A T L P R S Y M T Y A I A A

S O N S E H I C P I F H R P W F

P L G C S M N L T N A N E V O C

B W F K S H G B I G U P Y C R S

N I J U E P I Q O H T R A E I W

C M X K D M A D E Z K P D T P G

Acts, chapter 3 verse 25

You are the sons of the prophets and of the covenant that God made with you fathers, saying to Abraham, ‘And in your offspring all the families of the earth will be blessed.’

A	D	F	R	E	S	M	O	E	I	S	Y	O	U	R	F
C	B	T	M	J	W	T	F	L	M	T	R	A	P	M	G
R	E	H	O	R	C	B	T	A	E	R	D	Y	N	I	S
E	D	G	F	I	A	E	I	P	Z	V	O	N	A	F	H
M	O	I	D	E	W	T	A	T	S	U	G	A	S	T	E
R	M	S	C	U	L	S	H	R	D	F	J	H	D	U	C
P	H	B	A	V	J	O	G	E	P	N	E	T	S	I	L
G	E	Y	G	O	D	B	R	K	R	J	V	Y	N	A	R
P	K	I	X	I	N	A	E	I	H	R	F	O	D	J	G
B	W	F	A	T	S	V	D	M	G	U	P	R	C	E	N
C	N	L	W	H	E	T	H	E	R	H	O	W	H	K	Y
X	O	G	M	T	P	U	R	J	B	M	T	D	V	S	B

Acts, chapter 4 verse 19

Whether it is right in the sight of God to listen to you rather than God you must judge.

highlights from **ACTS … chapter 4**

1 DOWN: The Sadducees, the priests, and the captain of the temple arrested Peter and John for teaching, and proclaiming in Jesus the R ___ ___ ___ ___ ___ ___ ___ ___ ___ ___ ___ of the dead, and many had believed including about five thousand men (Acts 4:1-4)

2 ACROSS: The next day the elders, scribes, the high priest and all his family gathered and inquired, "By what power or by what N ___ ___ ___ do you do this?" (Acts 4:5-7)

3 ACROSS: Peter, filled with the Holy S ___ ___ ___ ___ ___ said "The crippled man by the temple was healed by the name of Jesus Christ of Nazareth, whom you crucified, whom God raised from the dead." (Acts 4:8-10)

4 ACROSS: "This Jesus is the stone that was rejected by you builders, which has become the cornerstone. And there is no other name under H ___ ___ ___ ___ ___ by which we must be saved." (Acts 4:11-12)

5 DOWN: They were astonished by the boldness of such ordinary men as Peter and John, but seeing the H ___ ___ ___ ___ ___ man standing beside them, they had nothing to say in opposition. (Acts 4:13-14)

6 DOWN: They commanded them to leave the council and conferred with one another; "We cannot deny what has happened. Let us warn them to S ___ ___ ___ speaking in this name, so that the word spreads no more among the people." (Acts 4:15-18)

7 ACROSS: On receiving the warning Peter and John answered, "You judge whether it is right that we L ___ ___ ___ ___ ___ to you rather than God. We cannot but speak of what we have seen and heard." (Acts 4:19-20)

8 DOWN: They threatened them, then let them go, for all the people were praising God for the man's healing. When Peter and John returned and reported all that happened to their friends, they all P ___ ___ ___ ___ ___ ___ God. (Acts 4:21-30)

9 ACROSS: As they had prayed, the place in which they were gathered was shaken, and they were all F ___ ___ ___ ___ ___ with the Holy Spirit and continued to speak the word of God with boldness. (Acts 4:31)

10 ACROSS: Now all who believed were of one heart and soul, having everything in common. The apostles' testified of the Lord Jesus' resurrection and great G ___ ___ ___ ___ was upon them all. (Acts 4:32-34)

11 DOWN: Those who had houses and land S ___ ___ ___ them and the proceeds were distributed to each as any had need. Joseph (aka Barnabas, which means son of encouragement) a Levite from Cyprus, sold his field and brought the money to the apostles. (Acts 4:34-37)

(To be continued …)

RESURRECTION; NAME; SPIRIT; HEAVEN; HEALED;
STOP; LISTEN; PRAISED; FILLED; GRACE; SOLD

ACTS

Chapter 4

highlights from **ACTS … chapter 5**

1 DOWN: Joseph sold his field and brought the money to the A __ __ __ __ __ __ __. But Ananias and his wife Sapphira when they sold their property kept some of the proceeds and presented the rest to the apostles as if that was all they got. (Acts 4:37-5:2)

2 ACROSS: Peter said to Ananias, "It was at your disposal both when it was unsold, and after it was sold; you have not L __ __ __ to man but to God. When Ananias heard these words, he fell dead. Then the young men wrapping him, took him and buried him. (Acts 5:3-6)

3 ACROSS: After about three hours Sapphira came, not knowing what had happened. When she also lied, Peter said, "How is it you have agreed together to test the Spirit of the Lord? Those who buried your H __ __ __ __ __ __ will carry you out. Immediately she too fell dead. Great fear came upon the whole church. (Acts 5:10-11)

4 ACROSS: The apostles did many signs and wonders as they gathered in Solomon's portico. Though none dared join them, the P __ __ __ __ __ held them in high esteem, and multitudes were believing and being added to the Lord. (Acts 5:12-14)

5 ACROSS: People, from around Jerusalem, brought the sick and those with unclean spirits so that even Peter's S __ __ __ __ __ might fall on some of them and heal them. (Acts 5:15-16)

6 DOWN: The high priest put them in prison, but during the night an A __ __ __ __ of the Lord freed them, commanding them to go to the temple and preach. (Acts 5:17-21)

7 ACROSS: Next day, when the high priest council summoned them, they were told that they were in the temple teaching. The officers went for them, and when questioned, Peter responded, "We must obey God R __ __ __ __ __ than men." (Acts 5:22-29)

8 DOWN: "God raised Jesus, whom you killed, and exalted Him as S __ __ __ __ __ to give repentance to Israel and forgiveness of sins. And we are witnesses of these things, and so is the Holy Spirit whom God has given to those who obey Him". (Acts 5:30-32)

9 ACROSS: Gamaliel, a Pharisee on the council, put the apostles out for a while, and advised the others to "Keep away from these men for if what they are doing is of man it will fail; but if it is of God, you will not be A __ __ __ to overthrow them." (Acts 4:33-39)

10 DOWN: The council took his advice, and calling them in, ordered them to be B __ __ __ __ __, and charging them not to speak in the name of Jesus, let them go. They left rejoicing, and did not cease teaching and preaching in the temple that the Christ is Jesus. (Acts 5:40-42)

(To be continued …)

APOSTLES; LIED; HUSBAND; PEOPLE; SHADOW;
ANGEL; RATHER; SAVIOR; ABLE; BEATEN

ACTS

Chapter 5

A Z N A H T D W E V F U D T H S

I R J Q K P R O M N S H A Z D W

B Y F U L O P L K Q G K G A R N

R E C V A V D H Q E V M U S T V

S K U N R C O E J F W A N E Q C

P F D A E B Y A R B G O D L P O

M Y W I T H E W N E M W I T U B

U K P Z E Z G U P H W X F S C E

G F W J P B E D O V K S Q O F Y

L S R E H T A R W H K U N P G C

B K L W J S L Q N V H O W A K E

A O G E T P U R J B M T F V S B

Acts, chapter 5 verse 29

But Peter and the apostles answered, “We must obey God rather than men.”

T E H P O R P G J E D W K L O P
G V X Y D A Q R U Z A B A G R H
N K H C H I L D R E N J O E I N
D F D R S E T H A L V Z T L K V
S K U N W C P T I J W A R Z Q C
P F G A P B Y M S B D G A K P G
M B W I L L R W E X E W E K I L
U K P S A I D U M N I X H A C E
D F W E J F T J G V M S W V B A
L S I S G T Q C W T I U E P G R
Y K L O H S L Q N V H O W A K S
E A D M T F U R J B M E F V E I

Acts, chapter 6 verse 37

… Moses said to the children of Israel, "The Lord your God will raise up for you a prophet, like me from your brethren. Him you shall hear.

highlights from **ACTS … chapter 6**

1 DOWN: As the number of disciples increased, the Greek Jews complained that their widows were not given the same amount of D __ __ __ __ distribution as the Hebrew Jews. (Acts 6:1)

2 ACROSS: So the apostles held a meeting with them all, and decided that they would continue their focus on prayer and M __ __ __ __ __ __ __ of the word, and seven godly and wise men, whose reputation was known by all, should be chosen to oversee the distributions. (Acts 6:2-4)

3 DOWN: The decision pleased everyone and they presented S __ __ __ __ __ __ (a man full of faith and the Holy Spirit), Philip, Prochorus, Nicanor, Timon, Parmenas and Nicolas (a proselyte from Antioch) to the apostles, who prayed and then laid hands of blessing on them. (Acts 6:5-6)

4 ACROSS: The Word of God spread and the number of disciples increased greatly. Among those who became obedient to the F __ __ __ __ were a great many priests. (Acts 6:7)

5 DOWN: Stephen, being full of faith and power, did many W __ __ __ __ __ __ and signs among the people. (Acts 6:8)

6 ACROSS: Then some of the group known as the Synagogue of Freedmen disputed with him but they could not stand against the wisdom and the S __ __ __ __ __ with which he spoke. (Acts 6:9-10)

6 DOWN: So they S __ __ __ __ __ __ __persuaded some men to say that they had heard Stephen speaking blasphemy against Moses and God. They continued to stir up the people, including the elders and the scribes; until the Jewish Leaders seized Stephen and brought him before the Council. (Acts 6:11-12)

7 DOWN: There they presented false W __ __ __ __ __ __ __ __ who said, "This man does not stop speaking against this holy place and the law. We heard him say that Jesus of Nazareth will destroy this place and change the customs that Moses gave us. (Acts 6:13-14)

8 ACROSS: All those sitting on the council stared at Stephen for they saw in his face the appearance of an A __ __ __ __. (Acts 6:15)

(To be continued …)

DAILY; MINISTRY; STEPHEN; FAITH; WONDERS;
SPIRIT; SECRETLY; WITNESSES; ANGEL

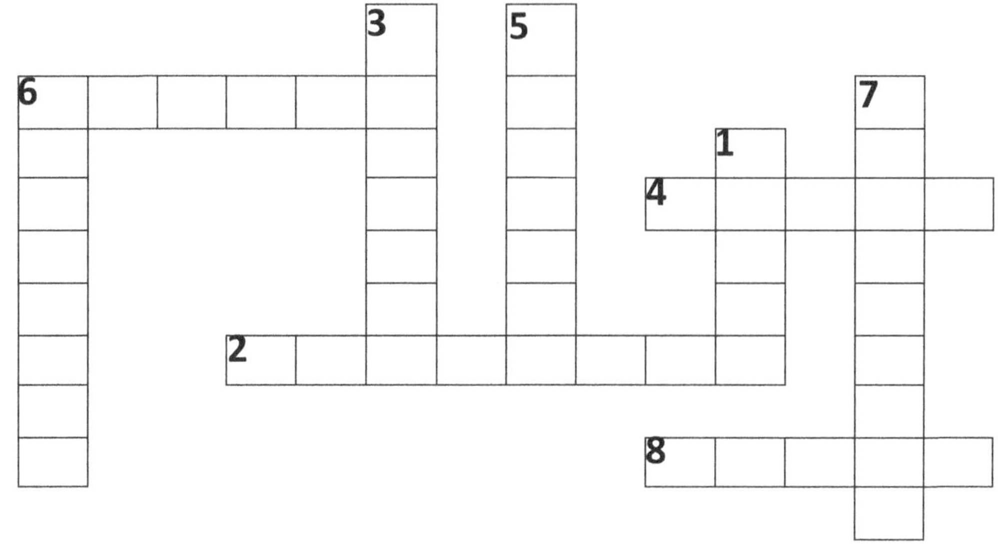

ACTS

Chapter 6

highlights from **ACTS … chapter 7a**

1 DOWN: On hearing the testimony of the F __ __ __ __ witnesses the high priests asked Stephen, "Are these things so?" (Acts 7:1)

2 ACROSS: And Stephen said, "Brothers and Fathers, Listen to me. A __ __ __ __ __ __ left his homeland, heading for a land God promised to show him. He stopped in Haran and after his father's death God moved him on to the land where you are now living." (Acts 7:2-4)

3 DOWN: "Though Abraham had no C __ __ __ __at the time, God promised the land to his offspring. God told him before they came to worship in this place, his offspring would be enslaved for 400 years in a land where they were sojourners." (Acts 7:5-7)

4 DOWN: "God gave circumcision as a covenant, and when Abraham became father to Isaac, he circumcised him on the 8th day. Isaac became F __ __ __ __ __ to Jacob, and Jacob became father to the 12 patriarchs, who being jealous of their brother Joseph sold him into Egypt." (Acts 7:8-9)

5 ACROSS: "God rescued Joseph from the afflictions of his slavery and gave him wisdom and favor with Pharaoh. A F __ __ __ __ __ came and Jacob hearing there was food in Egypt sent our fathers there. On their 2nd visit Joseph made himself known to his brothers." (Acts 7:10-13)

6 DOWN: "Joseph sent for his father and family, all 75 persons, to come to Egypt where Jacob lived until he died and was carried back to be buried at Shechem. The people increased in Egypt and there came a time of a pharaoh who did not know of J __ __ __ __ __ and who dealt shrewdly with our people." (Acts 7:14-18)

7 ACROSS: "It was during this time that M __ __ __ __ was born and eventually adopted by Pharaoh's daughter." (Acts 7:19-22)

8 DOWN: "When he was 40 years old, he struck down an Egyptian who was oppressing one of his Hebrew brethren. Moses fled to M __ __ __ __ __ when he realized his deed had been discovered. There he became father to 2 sons." (Acts 7:23-29)

9 ACROSS: "After 40 years God spoke to Moses in a flame of fire in a bush. 'Take the sandals off your feet for the place where you are standing is H __ __ __ ground.'" (Acts 7:30-33)

10 DOWN: "'I have surely seen the afflictions of my people in E __ __ __ __ and I have come to deliver them. Come now, I will send you to Egypt.'" (Acts 7:34)

(To be continued …)

FALSE; ABRAHAM; CHILD; FATHER; FAMINE;
JOSEPH; MOSES; MIDIAN; HOLY; EGYPT

ACTS

Chapter 7a

D F A Q G P L D H C B U I D M N

R T V W B I O O N X N Z N X E F

M N F A D L V G K D J A M C S L

F O B P P C R I E C H Q R U I T

Q I S L U O M R N Z W Y L X H O

N T E X N S S K Y G B Z E I N N

T A H G S T E S J V K W O U L D

U V N E A R H S E E G V D Y A E

B L D N Y P T P U S Z Q U T E R

J A D L G X O D E S O P P U S D

W S J U F P I Q L T F M V X I T

C M X K R B R O T H E R S D H G

Acts, chapter 7 verse 25

He (Moses) supposed that his brothers would understand that God was giving them salvation by his hand but they did not understand.

D F A Q G P W D H C B U I D M D
R T V E B L O O N X T Z N X L F
M N F A K L V G K D A A M I S O
F O B P P A U I E C H O U S E R
D R O L U O M O N Z W B L X H O
N T E X N S S K Y I R Z N I N P
T A H G S T E S L V K W O U L D
U V N E A R H L E E G V T Y A S
B L D N Y P T E U S Z Q U T E D
J A I L S X O D E S O P P U S N
W S D U F P I Q L T F M Y X I A
C M X K R B R O T H E R S D K H

Acts, chapter 7 verse 49b

"What kind of house will you build for Me?",
says the Lord, "or what is the place of my rest?
Did not my hands make all these things?"

highlights from **ACTS ... chapter 7b**

1 ACROSS: On hearing the testimony of the F __ __ __ __ witnesses the high priests asked Stephen, "Are these things so?" (Acts 7:1)

2 DOWN: And S__ __ __ __ __ __ continued in his response, "Moses, who God's angel appeared to in the burning bush, they rejected saying, 'Who made you a ruler and a judge?'" (Acts 7:35)

3 ACROSS: "This Moses led them performing signs and wonders in Egypt, at the Red Sea, and in the W __ __ __ __ __ __ __ __ __ for 40 years." (Acts 7:36)

4 ACROSS: "This Moses told the Israelites God would raise up a prophet like himself. This Moses who led us out of Egypt, we do not know what became of him. He gave them living oracles he received on Mount Sinai but our fathers refused to O __ __ __, instead asking Aaron to make for them an idol." (Acts 7:37-41)

5 DOWN: "Our fathers brought the tent of the tabernacle with them when under J __ __ __ __ __ they took the land from the nations God drove out before them. David asked for a dwelling place for the God of Jacob, but it was Solomon who built it." (Acts 7:42-47)

6 ACROSS: "Yet the Most H __ __ __ does not dwell in houses made by hands; as the prophet says, 'Heaven is my throne, and earth my footstool.'" (Acts 7:48-50)

7 DOWN: "And just as your F __ __ __ __ __ __ did, so you too always resist the Holy Spirit. They killed those who foretold the coming of the Righteous One and you have now betrayed and murdered Him." (Acts 7:51-53)

8 ACROSS: When the council heard Stephen saying these things they were enraged. But he full of the Holy Spirit gazed into H __ __ __ __ __ and saw the glory of God, and Jesus standing at the right hand of the Father. (Acts 7:54-57)

9 DOWN: They cast him out of the city and S __ __ __ __ __ him. And they laid their garments at the feet of a young man named Saul. (Acts 7:58)

10 ACROSS: As they were stoning Stephen he called out, "Lord Jesus, receive my spirit."; and falling to his knees he cried aloud, "Lord do N __ __ hold this sin against them," Then he fell asleep. (Acts 7:59-60)

(To be continued ...)

FALSE; STEPHEN; WILDERNESS; OBEY; JOSHUA;
HIGH; FATHERS; HEAVEN; STONED; NOT

ACTS

Chapter 7b

highlights from **ACTS … chapter 8**

1 ACROSS: Devout men buried Stephen and mourned deeply for him. After which a great persecution of the C __ __ __ __ __ in Jerusalem began and all except the apostles scattered to the regions of Judea and Samaria. Saul, who had approved of Stephen's execution ravaged the church, dragging off men and women to prison. (Acts 8:1-3)

2 DOWN: Those who left Jerusalem went about P __ __ __ __ __ __ __ __ the Word. Philip proclaimed Christ in Samaria and when the crowds saw the miracles done by him, they paid rapt attention to the Word. So there was much joy in the city. (Acts 8:4-8)

3 ACROSS: A magician named Simon, who had previously been amazing the people of the city and saying that he himself was someone great believed and was B __ __ __ __ __ __ __ along with all the others, when they heard the good news of the kingdom of God and the name of Jesus Christ, preached by Philip. (Acts 8:9-13)

4 ACROSS: When the apostles in Jerusalem heard, they sent Peter and John, who came and prayed and laid hands on them and they received the Holy S __ __ __ __ __. Simon seeing this, offered the apostles money saying, "Give me this power also so that anyone on whom I lay hands may receive the Holy Spirit." (Acts 8:14-19)

5 DOWN: But Peter said to him, "May your silver perish with you because you thought you could obtain the gift of God with money. R __ __ __ __ __ and pray that, if possible, the intent of your heart may be forgiven." Simon answered, "Pray for me to the Lord that nothing of what you have said, may come upon me. (Acts 8:20-24)

6 ACROSS: After they testified and preached the Word of the L __ __ __ there, they returned to Jerusalem, having preached the gospel to many villages of the Samaritans (Acts 8:25)

7 DOWN: Now an angel told Philip to go south, to the desert place on the road from Jerusalem to Gaza. An E __ __ __ __ __ __ __ __ eunuch, a court official to Candace, queen of the Ethiopians was there, seated in his chariot, reading the prophet Isaiah. He was returning from worship in Jerusalem (Acts 8:26-28)

8 ACROSS: And the Spirit told Philip to approach him. So Philip ran to him and asked if he understood what he was R __ __ __ __ __ __. "How can I, unless someone guides me?" he replied, inviting Philip to join him. Philip used the passage from Isaiah to explain the good news about Jesus. (Acts 8:29-35)

9 ACROSS: As they C __ __ __ __ __ __ __ __ along the road they saw some water and the eunuch said, "Here is water, what prevents me from being baptized? He stopped the chariot and Philip and the eunuch went down into the water and he was baptized. (Acts 8:36-38)

10 ACROSS: When they came up O __ __ of the water, the Spirit of the Lord carried Philip away and the eunuch saw him no more, and went on his way rejoicing. Next Philip found himself in Azotus and he preached to all the towns along the way until he came to Caesarea. (Acts 8:39)

(To be continued …)

CHURCH; PREACHING; BAPTIZED; SPIRIT; REPENT;
LORD; ETHIOPIAN; READING; CONTINUED; OUT

ACTS

Chapter 8

D F A Q G P W D H C N U I D S D

R T V E B D O O G X T E N X U F

M N F A K L V B K D A A W I S O

F O B N P A S S A G E O U S E R

D R O L H W M O C Z W B L X J O

S T E X I S S K Y R R Z D I N P

E A H T L T E S L V I W L U L D

U V H E I R H L E E G P O Y A S

J A D N P Y T E U S Z Q T T E D

T L I L S X O D E S O E S U S N

W S D U F P I Q L T F M Y X R A

C M T U O B A O T H E R S D K E

Acts, chapter 8 verse 35

Then Philip began with that very passage of Scripture and told him the good news about Jesus.

D F A Q G P W D H C N U N O S D
R S V E B D O O G X T D H X U F
M E F A K L V B K D E A W I P O
F U B N P A S S A H T A H T E R
D G O L H W M O C Z W B L X J O
S O E X V S S A Y R R Z D I N P
E G R T L C E S L V I W L U L D
U A C E O R H L E B G P O Y A S
J N D N P Y T R U R Z Q T T E D
T Y G L S X R D I J O G S U S N
W S D U F P I Q L S F N O X R A
C M T O G B A O E H T R S D K E

Acts, chapter 9 verse 20

Immediately he (Saul) preached Christ in the synagogues, that He is the Son of God.

highlights from **ACTS … chapter 9**

1 ACROSS: Saul continued his threats and murder of the disciples in Jerusalem. Then he asked the high P __ __ __ __ __ to send him to Damascus so that he might bring back and imprison in Jerusalem any disciples of the Way he might find there. (Acts 9:1-2)

2 DOWN: As he approached D __ __ __ __ __ __ __, a light from heaven struck him to the ground. He heard a voice saying to him, "Saul, Saul, why are you persecuting me?"; and he asked, "Who are you, Lord?" Then the Lord said, "I am Jesus, whom you are persecuting. Get up and go into the city, and you will be told what you must do." (Acts 9:3-5)

3 ACROSS: The men with S __ __ __ were speechless at hearing the voice but seeing no one. Saul was led by the hand into Damascus as he was blinded. He was there unable to see for three days and he neither ate nor drank during that time. (Acts 9:6-9)

4 DOWN: Meanwhile a D __ __ __ __ __ __ __ in Damascus named Ananias heard from the Lord in a vision. He was told that Saul was at Judas' house on Straight Street, and that he was praying and had received a vision that Ananias was coming to lay hands on him and restore his sight. (Acts 9:10-12)

5 ACROSS: Ananias was at first hesitant because of Saul's reputation but the Lord assured him saying that Saul had been chosen to bring the name of J __ __ __ __ to the non-Jews. (Acts 9:13-16)

6 ACROSS: Ananias went and laid H __ __ __ __ on Saul. Immediately something like scales fell from his eyes. His sight was restored and he was filled with the Holy Spirit; and he arose and was baptized. (Acts 9:17-18)

7 DOWN: Saul spent some days with the disciples in Damascus and immediately started preaching in the synagogues that Jesus was the Christ, the S __ __ of God. This amazed those who heard as they knew of his original reason for coming to Damascus (Acts 9:19-22)

8 DOWN: Many days passed and then the Jewish leaders plotted to kill him; but Saul discovered the P __ __ __ and the disciples helped him escape to Jerusalem. The disciples in Jerusalem did not trust him at first but Barnabas took him to the apostles and recounted all Saul's experiences in Damascus. (Acts 9:23-27)

9 ACROSS: Saul continued speaking boldly about Jesus and the Greek speaking Jewish leaders in Jerusalem tried to kill him, but the disciples helped him E __ __ __ __ __ to Tarsus. (Acts 9:28-30)

10 DOWN: Meanwhile Peter was preaching throughout all parts of the country. In Lydda he healed Aeneas, who had been bedridden for 8 years; in Joppa he raised Dorcas from the dead. Many B __ __ __ __ __ __ __ on the Lord when they saw these miracles. (Acts 9:31-43)

(To be continued …)

PRIEST; DAMASCUS; SAUL; DISCIPLE; JESUS;
HANDS; SON; PLOT; ESCAPE; BELIEVED

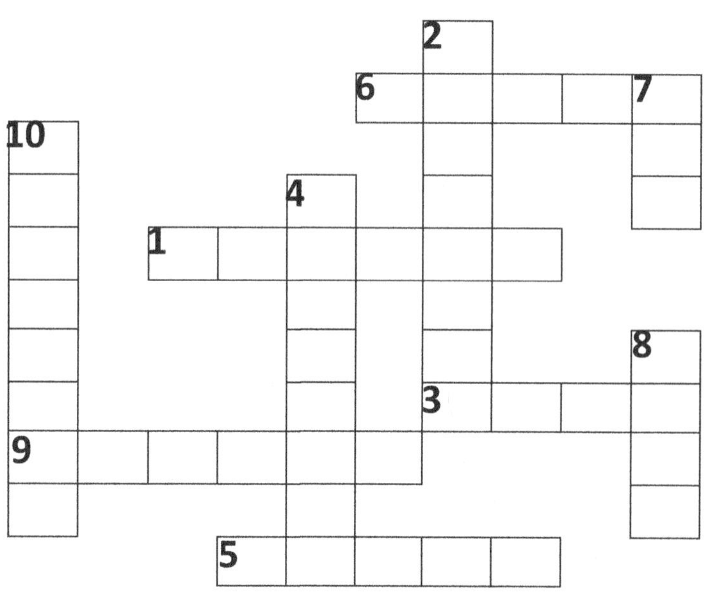

ACTS

Chapter 9

highlights from **ACTS ... chapter 10**

1 ACROSS: One day at 3p.m. a devout, God-fearing centurion who lived in Caesarea had a vison from God. An angel said to him, "Your P __ __ __ __ __ __ and generous gifts to the people have been noticed by God. Send men to Joppa and bring Simon Peter here. He is staying with Simon the tanner whose house is by the sea." (Acts 10:1-6)

2 DOWN: So Cornelius sent two of his servants along with a devout soldier to J __ __ __ __. The next day, as they were approaching the city, Simon Peter had a vision. He was praying at about noon when he fell into a trance and saw what looked like a sheet being let down by its corners from heaven. It had all kinds of animals in it and a voice said, "Rise Peter, kill and eat." (Acts 10:7-13)

3 ACROSS: Peter replied that he had never E __ __ __ __ anything declared common or unclean by Kosher law, but the voice responded, "What God has made clean, do not call common." This was repeated three times and then the sheet was taken back up. (Acts 10:14-16)

4 DOWN: While Peter was thinking about the meaning of the V __ __ __ __ __, the Spirit told him that three men were outside looking for him. Accompany them to Caesarea, just as they will ask. So Peter invited them to stay the night and the next day he and some of the brothers from Joppa headed for Caesarea. (Acts 10:17-24)

5 ACROSS: Cornelius was expecting them and had called together some relatives and close friends. On seeing Peter, he fell at his feet to W __ __ __ __ __ __ him, but Peter lifted him up saying, "Stand up for I too am a man.", and he told Cornelius of his vision. Cornelius in turn told Peter of his vision. (Acts 10:24-33)

6 DOWN: Then Peter declared, "Indeed God shows no P __ __ __ __ __ __ __ __ __, but in every nation anyone who fears Him and does what is right is acceptable." (Acts 10:34-38)

7 DOWN: "We are W __ __ __ __ __ __ __ __ to all that Jesus did and that he was killed but God raised him up on the third day. God chose even us to eat and drink with him after He rose from the dead." (Acts 10:39-42)

8 DOWN: And He commanded us to preach to the people and testify that He was ordained by God to be the Judge of the living and the dead. All the prophets bear witness that those who B __ __ __ __ __ __ in Him will receive remission of sins. (Acts 10:42-43)

9 ACROSS: While Peter was speaking, the H __ __ __ Spirit fell on all those who heard him. The Jews who had come with him were astonished that non-Jews also received the gift of the Holy Spirit as they heard then speak with tongues and magnify God. (Acts 10:44-46)

10 ACROSS: Then Peter answered, "Can anyone F __ __ __ __ __ these who have received the Holy Spirit to be baptized in water, just as we have been baptized? So he commanded them to be baptized. Then they asked him to stay a few days. (Acts 10:47-48)

(To be continued ...)

PRAYERS; JOPPA; EATEN; VISION; WORSHIP;
PARTIALITY; WITNESSES; BELIEVE; HOLY; FORBID

ACTS

Chapter 10

D F A Q G P W D H C N U N O S D
R S V E B D K P G X T L H X U F
M E F A K L V O A D L A W I P O
F U B N P A D S A A T A H T E R
D G T A H W M R C Z W B L X J O
S E E X V S S A Y R R Z A I N P
E G S T L C E S L V I W L N L D
U A C N O R H L E B G P L O A S
J N D N A Y T R U T T S U M E D
T Y G L O E R D I J O G S M S N
W S D U F P L Q L S F N J O R A
C M T H G B A C E H T R S C K E

Acts, chapter 10 verse 15

What God has cleansed you must not call common.

S N A I T S I R H C N U N O D S

R S V E B D K P G X T L H X U E

M A F A K L V O A D L A W I P L

F U E N P A D S T H G U A T E P

D G T Y N A M R C Z W B L X J I

S E E X V S S A Y R R Z D I D C

E H M T L C E S L V I W L O N S

T A C A O R H L H C O I T N A I

J N D N N Y T U U T T S U M E D

P Y G L O E R D R J O G S M S N

W S D U D E L L A C F N J O R Y

C M T H G W E R E T H R H C K E

Acts, chapter 11 verse 26

For a whole year they (Barnabas and Saul a.k.a. Paul) met with the church and taught a great many people. And in Antioch the disciples were first called Christians.

highlights from **ACTS ... chapter 11**

1 ACROSS: Now the A __ __ __ __ __ __ __ and the brethren all throughout Judea heard of the conversion of the non-Jews. On Peter's return to Jerusalem a clique of circumcised men accosted him saying, "You went and ate with uncircumcised men." (Acts 11:1-3)

2 DOWN: Then Peter told them of his vision; that three times a sheet full of un-Kosher food descended from heaven, and the V __ __ __ __ from heaven declared, "What God has made clean, do not call common." (Acts 11:4-10)

3 DOWN: He told them of the Holy Spirit's directing him to go with the men sent to fetch him from Caesarea; and there hearing from Cornelius about the angel who had told him Peter who would declare the M __ __ __ __ __ __ of how to be saved. (Acts 11:11-14)

4 ACROSS: Peter continued by telling them that when he saw the Holy Spirit fall on them, just as it had done on us at the beginning, he R __ __ __ __ __ __ __ __ __ Jesus' words, "John baptized with water, but you will be baptized with the Holy Spirit." (Acts 11:15-16)

5 DOWN: "Who was I, that I could stand in God's way", Peter declared. And when the others heard these things, they had nothing more to say, but glorified God that He had granted, also to the non-Jews, repentance that leads to L __ __ __. (Acts 11:17-18)

6 DOWN: Those who had fled Jerusalem after Stephen's death had been preaching only to the Jews wherever they went. But some of them who were originally from Cyprus and Cyrene, preached about Jesus to the Greeks in Antioch. A great many believed and turned to the L __ __ __. (Acts 11:19-21)

7 DOWN: When the news reached the church in Jerusalem, they sent Barnabas to Antioch. Barnabas was a good man, full of the Holy Spirit and of faith. When he arrived in Antioch and saw the G __ __ __ __ of God, he was glad and exhorted them all to remain faithful to the Lord, with steadfast purpose. (Acts 11:22-24)

8 ACROSS: A great many people were added to the Lord. So, Barnabas went to Tarsus and brought Saul back with him to Antioch. They stayed there for a Y __ __ __ teaching a great many people. It was in Antioch that the disciples were first called Christians. (Acts 11:25-26)

9 DOWN: In these days prophets came down from Jerusalem. One, named Agabus prophesied that there would be a great F __ __ __ __ __ all over the world. (Acts 11:27-28)

10 ACROSS: So the disciples decided to send relief to the brothers living in Judea. E__ __ __ contributed according to his ability and they sent it to the elders by the hands of Barnabas and Saul. (Acts 11:29-30)

(To be continued ...)

APOSTLES; VOICE; MESSAGE; REMEMBERED;
LIFE; LORD; GRACE; YEAR; FAMINE; EACH

ACTS

Chapter 11

highlights from **ACTS ... chapter 12**

1 DOWN: Herod, the king began persecuting some who belonged to the Church. His killing with the sword of John's B __ __ __ __ __ __, James, pleased the Jewish leaders, so he proceeded to arrest Peter. (Acts 12:1-3)

2 ACROSS: This happened during the holidays of The Unleavened B __ __ __ __. He put Peter in prison where he was guarded by four (4) squadrons of soldiers. Herod intended to delay bringing him out for trial before the people until after all the Passover celebrations. (Acts 12:3-4)

3 ACROSS: While Peter was being kept in prison, the church was earnestly P __ __ __ __ __ __ to God for him. On the very night that Herod planned for Peter's trial, he was being kept bound with two (2) chains, sleeping between two (2) soldiers, and there were sentries guarding the door of the prison. (Acts 12:5-6)

4 DOWN: So Peter thought it was a vision when an angel of the Lord stood next to him and a light shone in the cell. The A __ __ __ __ said, "Get up quickly". And the chains fell off his hands. Peter obeyed the angel's instructions to get dressed and follow him. (Acts 12:7-9)

5 DOWN: They passed both guards, and when they came to the city's iron gate it O __ __ __ __ __ for them of its own accord. They passed along one street and then the angel left him. When Peter came to himself, he realized that the Lord had sent an angel to rescue him. (Acts 12:10-11)

6 ACROSS: He went to Mary's house. (She was John Mark's mother). Many were gathered there praying and when Rhoda, the servant girl, heard a K __ __ __ __ __ __ __ she went to the gate to see who it was. But when she saw that it was Peter, overcome with joy she rushed back in to tell them, instead of letting Peter in. (Acts 12:12-15)

7 ACROSS: Well, they didn't B __ __ __ __ __ __ her, but when the knocking persisted, they went themselves and saw it was indeed Peter. They were amazed, but he signaled them to be quiet, as he reported all that had happened and told them to tell James and the other brothers. He then departed to another place. (Acts 12:16-17)

8 ACROSS: At daybreak the soldiers were, to say the least, disturbed over Peter's disappearance. Herod ordered a S __ __ __ __ __, but Peter could not be found so he ordered that the sentries should be put to death and then he left Judea to spend some time in Caesarea. (Acts 12:18-19)

9 DOWN: Herod had been angry with the people of Tyre and Sidon. But they wanted to appease him as their people depended on the king's country for their food supply. So, on an appointed day as Herod sat on his T __ __ __ __ __ and delivered an oration to them they shouted," The voice of a god, not of a man!" (Acts 12:20-22)

10 DOWN: Immediately he was struck down and breathed his last, because he did not give God the G __ __ __ __. But the Word of God continued to spread. When Barnabas and Saul completed the delivery of the relief supplies to Jerusalem, they brought John Mark back with them. (Acts 12:23-25)

(To be continued ...)

BROTHER; BREAD; PRAYING; ANGEL; OPENED;
KNOCKING; BELIEVE; SEARCH; THRONE; GLORY

ACTS

Chapter 12

S N A I T M I R H C N U N O D S
R S V E B D U P G X T L H X U E
M A B A K L V L A D L A W I P L
F U E N P A D S T H D U A T E I
T G T Y N A M R C E W B L X J N
S E E X V S S A S R D Z D I D C
E H M T L C E A L V I B L O N R
T A C A O R E L H C O I M N G I
J N D J D R O W U T T S U T E D
P Y I N C E R D E J O G S M S N
W S A N D E L H A C F N J O R Y
D E I L P I T L U M H R H C K E

Acts, chapter 12 verse 24

But the Word of God increased and multiplied.

T O N I T M I R H C O U L D O S
R S B E B G U P G X T L H X U E
M A E A K U N L H D E A W I P Y
F U L N O A D I T H V U A T E I
T G I Y N A M R H E E B L X J F
D E E R F S S A S T R Y D I R C
E H V T L C E A L I Y B L O N R
A T E A W R E L H C O R M N G I
J N S H D R O W U T N S E T E D
P Y I O C E W D E J E G S V S N
W C R N D E L H A F C N J O E Y
H W A L P S E S O M H I H C K E

Acts, chapter 13 verse 39

By Him everyone who believes is freed from
everything from which you could not be freed
by the law of Moses.

highlights from ACTS … chapter 13

1 DOWN: The C _____ at Antioch under the direction of the Holy Spirit set Barnabas and Saul aside, laid their hands on them and sent them off. (Acts 13:1-3)

2 ACROSS: They traveled to Cyprus where they preached in Salamis and Paphos, assisted by John Mark. Bar-Jesus a magician and false P ______ there tried to dissuade the proconsul, of Paphos, Sergius Paulus, from hearing the Word. (Acts 13:4-8)

3 ACROSS: But Saul, filled with the Holy Spirit, strongly rebuked him saying "you will be blind for a time". Immediately a mist and darkness fell upon him. The consul, astonished at the teaching of the L ___, believed. (Acts 13:9-12)

4 ACROSS: John returned to Jerusalem, but Paul and the others continued on to Perga in Pamphylia. Then they went to Antioch in Pisidia., and on the S ______ they were asked to deliver a word of encouragement in the synagogue. (Acts 13:13-15)

5 DOWN: So Paul preached J ____. He told of God taking their ancestors to Egypt; of Moses and their delivery from slavery and the wilderness journey to Canaan; of Samuel the prophet and Saul the king; and then of king David whose offspring, Jesus, God brought to Israel as a Savior. (Acts 13:16-23)

6 ACROSS: He told of John proclaiming a baptism of repentance and of one coming whose sandals he was not worthy to untie; and that though the utterances of the prophets were read every Sabbath those in J ________ did not recognize him, and though they found nothing worthy of death, they asked Pilate to have him executed. (Acts 13:24-28)

7 DOWN: And when all that was written about him was fulfilled, they took him down from the tree and laid him in a tomb. But God R _____ him from the dead, and for many days he appeared to those who had come with him from Galilee to Jerusalem, and who are now his witnesses to the people. (Acts 13:29-31)

8 DOWN: Good News: God fulfilled his promise to the fathers, and as David spoke in the psalms the Holy One whom God raised up did not see corruption. Let it be known, brothers that through this man is forgiveness of sins; all who believe are freed from everything from which the law of M ____ could not free you. (Acts 13:32-39)

9 ACROSS: The people begged them to return the next Sabbath and the next Sabbath almost the whole city G _______ to hear the word of God. But the Jewish leaders filled with jealousy began to contradict and revile Paul. (Acts 13:40-45)

10 DOWN: Paul and Barnabas boldly stated, "We had to declare the Word of God to you first, but since you have rejected it we will now go to the non-Jewish peoples as the Lord has commanded." Many Gentiles believed, and the W ___ of the Lord was spreading throughout the whole region. (Acts 13:46-49)

11 ACROSS: When the Jewish leaders again stirred up persecution against Paul and Barnabas they shook the dust of their feet and continued on to Iconium. And the disciples were filled with J __ and with the Holy spirit. (Acts 13:50-52)

(To be continued …)

CHURCH; PROPHET; LORD; SABBATH; JESUS;
JERUSALEM; RAISED; MOSES; GATHERED; WORD; JOY

ACTS

Chapter 13

highlights from **ACTS … chapter 14**

1 DOWN: When Paul and Barnabas spoke at the S __ __ __ __ __ __ __ __ in Iconium a great many Jews and non-Jews believed the Gospel. Even though Jewish leaders there tried to poison the minds of the non-Jews, they continued for a long time, speaking boldly for the Lord, who bore witness with signs and wonders done by their hands. But the people of the city were divided in their opinion of the apostles. (Acts 14:1-4)

2 ACROSS: The A __ __ __ __ __ __ __ learned of a plan being hatched by both non-Jews and Jews to mistreat and stone them, so they fled to Lystra and Derbe, cities of Lycaonia in the surrounding country, and continued their preaching there. (Acts 14:5-7)

3 DOWN: There was a man in Lystra who was crippled from B __ __ __ __. Paul noticed how intently he listened and seeing that he had faith to be made well, said loudly "Stand upright on your feet!" And the man sprang up and began walking. (Acts 14:8-10)

4 DOWN: When the crowd saw what Paul had done, they declared, "The gods have come down to us in the L __ __ __ __ __ __ __ of men!" And the priest of the temple of Zeus that was at the gate of the city wanted to offer sacrifices along with the crowd. (Acts 14:11-13)

5 ACROSS: But when the apostles heard of this they rushed out in distress and cried out, "We are men, just like you, and we bring Good N __ __ __ that you should turn from these vain things to a living God who made all creation." (Acts 14:14-15)

6 DOWN: "Although in the P __ __ __ he has allowed all nations to do as they please, yet He still gave witness of who He is by giving rain and fruitful seasons satisfying your hearts with food and gladness." (Acts 14:16-17)

7 DOWN: Even with these W __ __ __ __ they were scarcely able to restrain them from offering sacrifices to them. But when Jewish leaders came from Antioch and Iconium, they persuaded the crowds to stone Paul, and presuming him to be dead, they dragged him out of the city. (Acts 14:18-19)

8 ACROSS: The D __ __ __ __ __ __ __ __ gathered around him and he was revived, entered the city and the next day along with Barnabas went on to Derbe. There they preached the Gospel, making many disciples before returning to Lystra, Iconiun, and Antioch to strengthen and encourage the disciples there. (Acts 14:20-22)

9 ACROSS: They told them of many tribulations through which we must enter the kingdom of God. And when they had appointed E __ __ __ __ __ for them in every church, they committed them to the Lord in whom they had believed. (Acts 14:22-23)

10 ACROSS: Passing through Pisidia, they preached in Perga of Pamphylia , then moved on to Attalia, sailing from there back to Antioch. In Antioch they were commended for the work they had done by God's grace. They reported on all that God had done and the D __ __ __ of faith He had opened to the non-Jews. (Acts 14:24-27)

11 DOWN: So, they stayed with the disciples there for quite a long T __ __ __. (Acts 14:28)

(To be continued …)

SYNAGOGUE; APOSTLES; BIRTH; LIKENESS; NEWS;
PAST; WORDS; DISCIPLES; ELDERS; DOOR; TIME

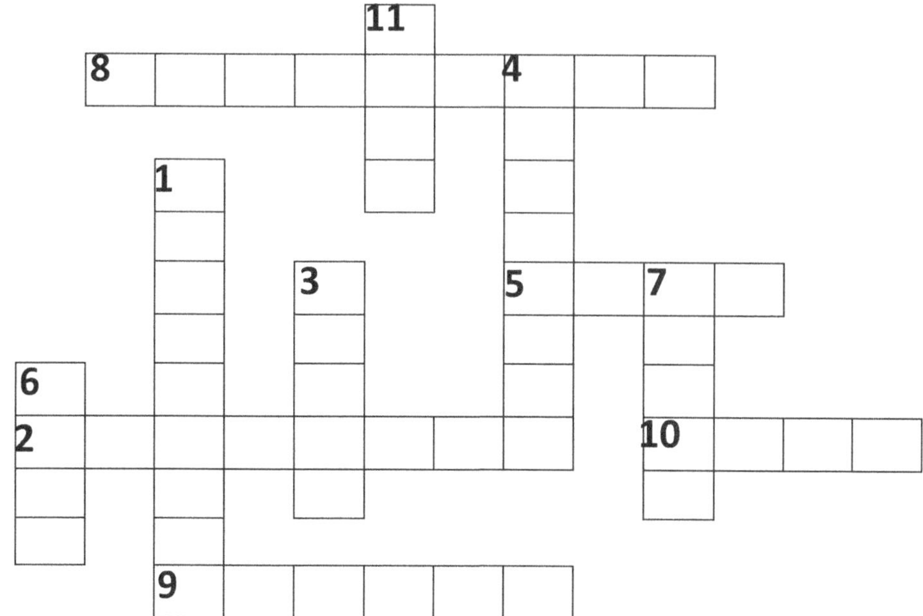

ACTS

Chapter 14

T O N I T M I R H C O U L D O S
R H B E B G U D G X T L H X U E
M A E A O D N L H D E A W I P Y
F U L Y O A E I T H V U A T E I
T D E N E P O C H E E B L X J F
D E E R F S S A L L R Y D I R C
E H V T L C D A S A Y B L O N R
A R E A W R E L H C R O M N G I
J N O H D R O W U T N E S T E D
P Y I O C E W D E J E G D V W N
W C R N D H T I A F C N J O E Y
H W A L P S E S O M H I H C K E

Acts, chapter 14 verse 27

And when they arrived and gathered the church together, they declared all that God had done with them, and how he had opened the door of faith to the Gentiles.

T O N I T M I R H C O U D R O L

R H B E B G U D E X F L H X U E

M G R A C E N L H D E A W I L Y

F U L O Y A E I T H V U A T E I

S L E N U E V E I L E B L X J F

U E L V F G S A L J R Y D I R C

S H S I L C H A C A Y B L O N R

E G P A W R E L V S R O M N G I

J N O H D R O C U E N E S T E D

P Y I O C E W D E J D G D V W N

W C R N D H T I A F C N J O E Y

H W A L P S E S L M H I H C K E

Acts, chapter 15 verse 11

But we believe that we will be saved through
the grace of the Lord Jesus, just as they will.

highlights from **ACTS … chapter 15**

1 DOWN: Some men came to Antioch from Judea, T __ __ __ __ __ __ __ the brethren that they could not be saved unless they were circumcised, according to the custom of Moses. After much dispute between them, and Paul and Barnabas, it was decided that they should take the matter to the apostles and elders in Jerusalem. (Acts 15:1-2)

2 ACROSS: On their way through Phoenicia and Samaria they reported the conversion of the non-Jews, bringing G __ __ __ __ joy to all the brethren. The apostles, elders and the church at Jerusalem received them and listened to all that they reported. Some Pharisees who now believed, voiced their agreement with circumcision. (Acts 15:3-5)

3 DOWN: The apostles and elders then met to consider the matter. Peter stood recounting his experience of God acknowledging the non-Jews, giving them the Holy Spirit and purifying their hearts by faith. "Why T __ __ __ God by putting a yoke on the neck of the disciples which neither our fathers nor we were able to bear?", he asked. (Acts 15:6-10)

4 ACROSS: "But we believe that through the G __ __ __ __ of the Lord Jesus Christ we shall be saved, just as they." Then they all kept silent as Paul and Barnabas reported on all that God had worked through them among the non-Jews. (Acts 15:11-12)

5 ACROSS: James then took the floor. He reminded them of Simon Peter's first visit to the non-Jews, and also of the words of the P __ __ __ __ __ __ __ declaring that the rebuilding of the tabernacle was "so that the rest of mankind may seek the Lord". "Therefore, I judge that we should not trouble the non-Jews who are turning to God" (Acts 15:14-15)

6 DOWN: James went on, "Let us write to them to abstain from things polluted by idols, from sexual I __ __ __ __ __ __ __ __ __, from things strangled, and from blood. For Moses has always had his preachers proclaiming in the synagogues every Sabbath in every city." (Acts 15:16-21)

7 ACROSS: The entire church in Jerusalem under the Holy Spirit's direction agreed, and sent a letter in the hands of Paul, Barnabas, Judas Barsabbas, Silas and several other leading men to Antioch. When the L __ __ __ __ __ from Jerusalem was read to the congregation in Antioch they rejoiced because of its encouragement. (Acts 15:22-31)

8 DOWN: Judas and Silas spent time E __ __ __ __ __ __ __ __ __ __ and strengthening the brothers in Antioch before returning to Jerusalem. Paul and Barnabas remained in Antioch with many others preaching and teaching the Word. (Acts 15:32-35)

9 ACROSS: After some time, Paul suggested to Barnabas that they re-visit the brothers in cities where they had previously preached the W __ __ __. Barnabas wanted to take John Mark along with them, but Paul was against the idea as John Mark had left them at Pamphylia, instead of going with them to continue the work. (Acts 15:36-38)

10 DOWN: This resulted in a S __ __ __ __ disagreement ending with Barnabas taking John Mark and sailing for Cyprus and Paul choosing Silas and heading for Syria and Cilia, having been commended by the brothers to the grace of the Lord. (Acts 15:39-41)

(To be continued …)

TEACHING; GREAT; TEST; GRACE; PROPHETS;
IMMORALITY; LETTER; ENCOURAGING; WORD; SHARP

ACTS

Chapter 15

highlights from **ACTS … chapter 16**

1 DOWN: At Lystra and Derbe, Paul met a well-respected disciple named T __ __ __ __ __ __; his mother was a Jewish believer and his father was Greek. Paul wanted Timothy to accompany him so he circumcised him, just because the Jews in those places knew that his father was not a Jew. (Acts 16:1-3)

2 ACROSS: They taught the churches in the cities that they travelled through to O __ __ __ __ __ __ the decisions reached by the apostles and elders in Jerusalem. So, their faith was strengthened and their numbers grew daily. (Acts 16:4-5)

3 DOWN: Directed by the Holy Spirit, they went through Phrygia and Galatia, passed Mysia and went to Troas. That night Paul had a V __ __ __ __ __ of a Macedonian man urging him to come and help them. We concluded that God wanted us to go there. (Acts 16:6-10)

4 ACROSS: We sailed directly to Samothrace, then Neapolis and then P __ __ __ __ __ __ __, a Roman colony and a leading city in Macedonia. After some days, on the Sabbath, we went to the riverside outside the city gate, supposing it would be a place of prayer. Lydia, who was from the city of Thyatira responded to the words spoken by Paul there, her heart being opened by the Lord. After she was baptized (and her household as well) she prevailed upon us to stay at her house. (Acts 16:11-15)

5 DOWN: For many days, as we went to the place of P __ __ __ __ __, a slave-girl, whose owners made much money from her powers of divination, followed us. Paul became greatly annoyed and commanded the spirit of divination to come out of her. (Acts 16:16-18)

6 DOWN: Well, when the owners saw that their money maker was no more, they dragged Paul and Silas before the magistrates in the marketplace. The magistrates gave orders for them to be beaten and thrown into P __ __ __ __ __. (Acts 16:19-23)

7 DOWN: They were placed in the secure inner prison with their F __ __ __ shackled. At midnight as the other prisoners listened to them praying and singing hymns, a sudden earthquake opened all the doors and everyone's shackles unfastened. (Acts 16:24-26)

8 DOWN: The jailer was about to kill himself when Paul cried out, "We are all here!" Trembling, he said to Paul and Silas, "Sirs, what must I do to be saved?" "Believe on the L __ __ __ Jesus." and they preached the Word of the Lord to him and his house. (Acts 16:27-32)

9 DOWN: Then the jailer washed their wounds, and he and his family were baptized. He took them to his H __ __ __ __ and provided them with food. He and his entire household rejoiced that he believed in God. (Acts 16:33-34)

10 ACROSS: At daybreak the magistrate sent O __ __ __ __ __ to release the prisoners. But Paul said, "We uncondemned Roman citizens were publicly beaten and imprisoned.". On hearing this the magistrates apologized and asked them to leave the city. After visiting and encouraging Lydia and the brethren, they left. (Acts 16:35-40)

(To be continued …)

TIMOTHY; OBSERVE; VISION; PHILIPPI; PRAYER;
PRISON; FEET; LORD; HOUSE; ORDERS

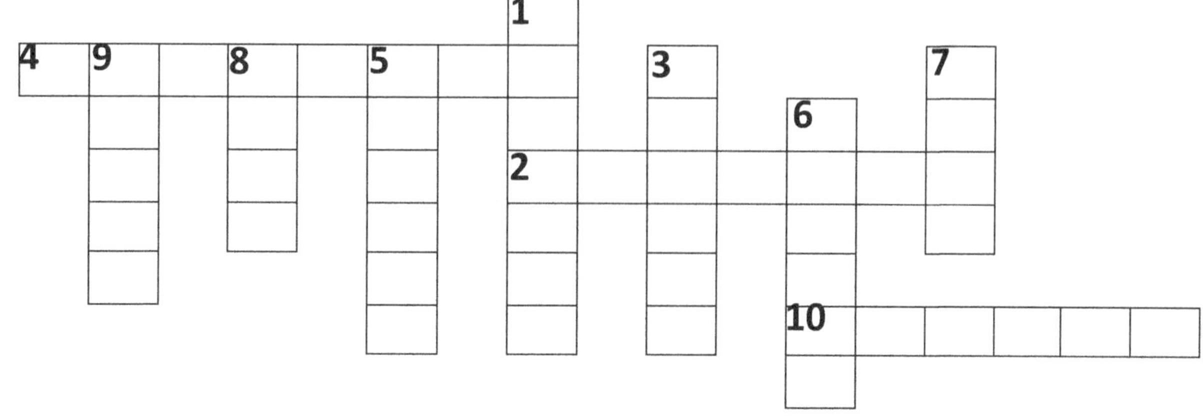

ACTS

Chapter 16

D F A Q G P L D H C B U S D M N
R T V W B I O O N X N Z N D E F
M N F A D L V G K D J A E C S L
F B O P P C R I E C H C R U I T
Q E S L U O E R N Z I Y L X H O
N L P X S N S K Y O B Z E A N N
T I H G T I F S J V K W T U L D
U E N I A R H E E A G V D Y A E
B V R N Y P R P U W Z Q U T E R
J E F L G X O D E I O P P U S D
W D J U F P I Q L T F M V X I T
C D L O H E S U O H E R S D H G

Acts, chapter 16 verse 34

… And he rejoiced along with his entire household that he had believed in God

D S A Q G P W D H C N U N O S U
R F C E B D O R E C E I V E D F
M E F R K L R B K D E A W X P O
F U B N I A D S A H T A H A E R
D G O D L P M O S Z W B L M J O
S O E A T S T A Y E R Z D I N P
E G R I J I E U L V N W L N L D
H A C L O R W L R B G R O I A S
T N D Y E H T R U E Z Q E N E D
I Y G B S X R D I J S G S G S N
W S D U F P I Q L S F N O X A A
C M T O G B A O E H T R S D K E

Acts, chapter 17 verse 11

They received the Word with all eagerness examining the Scriptures daily to see if these things were so.

highlights from **ACTS … chapter 17**

1 ACROSS: Having passed through Amphipolis and Apollonia, Paul, Silas and Timothy came to Thessalonica. As was his custom, Paul went to the synagogue and for three Sabbaths reasoned with them from the S __ __ __ __ __ __ __ __ __ that Jesus was the Christ. Among those persuaded were many devout Greeks, and notable women. (Acts 17:1-4)

2 DOWN: But some of the Jews who were not P __ __ __ __ __ __ __ __, recruited evil men from the marketplace to gather a mob who incited all the city to attack Jason's house where Paul and Silas had been staying. When they did not find them, they dragged Jason and some other brethren to the rulers of the city saying, "Those men who have turned the world upside down have come here too, and Jason has harbored them." (Acts 17:5-7)

3 ACROSS: They continued, "They are all acting contrary to the decrees of Caesar, saying there is another king, called J __ __ __ __." The crowd and the rulers of the city were troubled by these accusations. Then they made Jason and those with him post bond and let them go. (Acts 17:7-9)

4 ACROSS: The brethren responded by immediately sending Paul and Silas by night to Berea. The Jews in the synagogue at B __ __ __ __, being more noble than those in Thessalonica, eagerly receiving the Word and daily searched the Scriptures for themselves. Many therefore believed along with many notable Greeks. (Acts 17:10-12)

5 DOWN: But when the Jews from T __ __ __ __ __ __ __ __ __ __ __ heard, they came to Berea and stirred up the crowds there. The Berean brethren shipped Paul off to Athens. Silas and Timothy remained until it would be possible for them to join him. (Acts 9:17-18)

6 DOWN: The presence of so many idols in Athens, stirred Paul's spirit so that he reasoned in the synagogue with Jews and devout persons there, and daily with those who went to the marketplace. Some of the philosophers took him to their meeting place at Areopagus, where they were always spending their T __ __ __ telling and hearing of something new. (Acts 17:19-22)

7 DOWN: So Paul stood and spoke, "I notice you are very R __ __ __ __ __ __ __ __, having many objects of worship even including one 'to the unknown god'. The god who is unknown to you is the God who made the world and everything in it being Lord of heaven and earth. He made from one man every nation, that they should seek God. (Acts 17:22-27)

8 ACROSS: As God's offspring we ought not to think of the divine being as an image formed by the art and imagination of man. God has overlooked ignorance but now he commands all to R __ __ __ __ __, for he has fixed a day in which he will judge the world in righteousness by the Man he has appointed, whom he has raised from the dead. (Acts 17:28-31)

9 DOWN: Now when they heard mention of the resurrection some mocked, and some said they'd like to explore the topic more fully at another time. But some B __ __ __ __ __ __ __ and joined Paul as he went out from their midst. Among the believers was Dionysius and a woman named Damaris. (Acts 17:32-34)

(To be continued …)

SCRIPTURES; PERSUADED; JESUS; BEREA;
THESSALONICA; TIME; RELIGIOUS; REPENT; BELIEVED

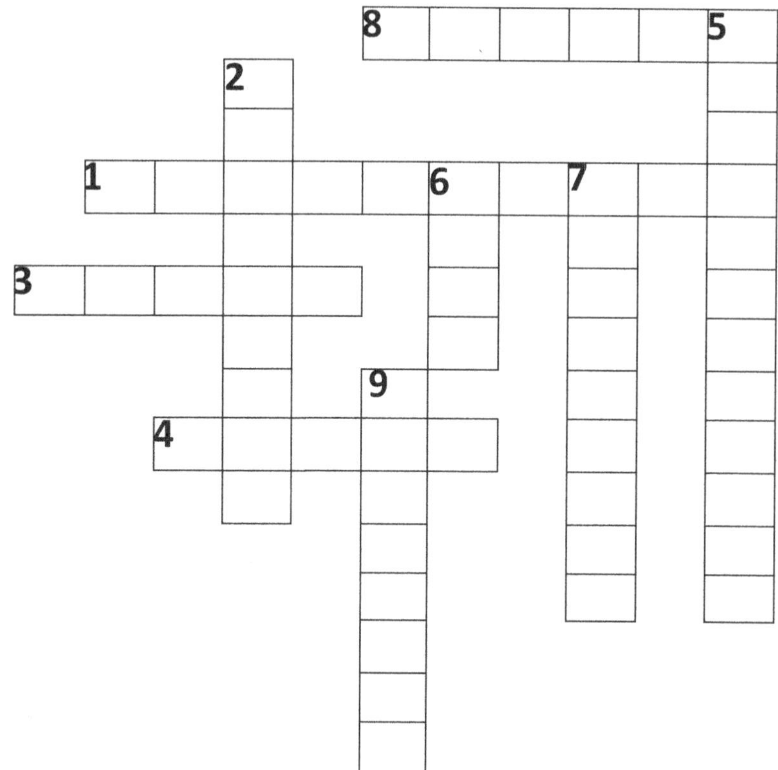

ACTS

Chapter 17

highlights from **ACTS … chapter 18**

1 ACROSS: Paul left Athens for Corinth and stayed there with Aquila and Priscilla, Jews from Pontus, Turkey but who had been L __ __ __ __ __ in Rome. When Claudius commanded all Jews to leave Rome they fled to Corinth. They were tentmakers, as was Paul. (Acts 18:1-3)

2 DOWN: Though Paul spent each Sabbath in the synagogue with both Jews and non-Jews, when Silas and Timothy arrived, they found him occupied, preaching to the Jews that Jesus was the C __ __ __ __ __. (Acts 18:4-5)

3 DOWN: The Jews opposed and reviled him, so shaking out his garments, he left there and went next door to the S __ __ __ __ __ __ __ __ to Titius Justus' house. Titius was a non-Jew and also a worshipper of God. (Acts 18:6-7)

4 ACROSS: Now Crispus, the ruler of the synagogue, together with his household, was a believer. In fact, many C __ __ __ __ __ __ __ __ __ __ had believed and were baptized. One night in a vision, the Lord told Paul, "Do not be afraid, go on speaking, I am with you and no one will harm you for I have many in the city who are my people." (Acts 18:8-10)

5 DOWN: Paul stayed in Corinth for a year and six months, teaching the word of God. The Jews made a united attack on him and brought him before the tribunal. But Gallio, the proconsul, said that persuading people to worship God contrary to their law is not a matter of wrong doing or a violent crime. And he R __ __ __ __ __ __ to make a judgement. (Acts 18:11-15)

6 DOWN: Gallio chased them out of the tribunal. Then they seized and beat Sosthenes, the ruler of the synagogue, but Gallio ignored it all. Paul stayed on in Corinth for quite a while before leaving for Syria, with P __ __ __ __ __ __ __ __ and Aquila. (Acts 18:16-18)

7 ACROSS: At Cenchreae he cut his hair as part of a vow that he had made. When they arrived at Ephesus, Paul left the others, taking a detour there to reason with the Jews in the synagogue. He declined their request that he stay longer but said, "I will return to you if God W __ __ __ __." And then he set sail from Ephesus. (Acts 18:17-21)

8 ACROSS When he landed in Caesarea, he went to the church there, before going on to Antioch, spending some time there, and then going from place to P __ __ __ __ as he traveled through Galatia and Phrygia, strengthening the disciples along the way. (Acts 18:22-23)

9 ACROSS: Apollos, an eloquent Jewish man from Alexandria came to Ephesus. Though competent in the S __ __ __ __ __ __ __ __ __, and fervently and accurately teaching about Jesus, he only knew the baptism of John. (Acts 18:24-25)

10 DOWN: On hearing him boldly speaking in the synagogue, Priscilla and Aquila privately gave him a more accurate explanation of the way of God. He desired to go to Achaia, so the brothers in Ephesus W __ __ __ __ ahead to them about him, so that when he arrived, he was welcomed. He was of great help to the believers there, publicly refuting the Jewish leaders, showing by the Scriptures that Jesus was the Christ. (Acts 18:26-28)

(To be continued …)

LIVING; CHRIST; SYNAGOGUE; CORINTHIANS; REFUSED;
PRISCILLA; WILLS; PLACE; SCRIPTURES; WROTE

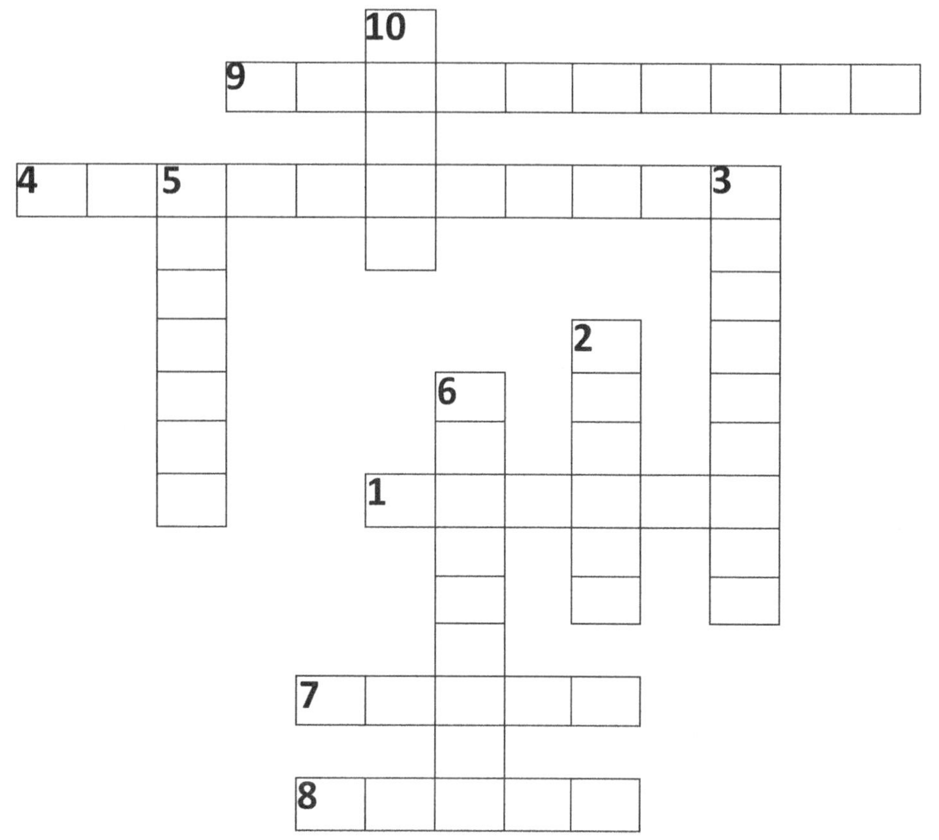

ACTS

Chapter 18

Y F A Q G P W D H C N U N O S D
L S V H I M D E N I A L P X E F
E E F A K L V O A D L A W I P O
T U B N P A D S O Q T A H T E T
A G T A R W M R C T U B S X J O
R E E X I S S A Y R R I O I N O
U G S T S C E S L V I W L N L K
C A C N C R H L E B G P L A A S
C S N B I Y D R U T E T O E E D
A I G D L E R E R O M G P M S N
W D F U L P L Q L S F S A O R A
C E Y L A T A R U C C A S N K E

Acts, chapter 18 verse 26

He (Apollos) began to speak boldly but when Priscilla and Aquila heard him, they took him aside and explained the way of God more accurately.

S	H	T	I	W	S	I	R	H	C	N	U	N	T	D	S
R	A	R	E	B	N	K	P	G	X	T	L	H	X	U	E
M	N	F	A	K	R	A	O	E	D	L	A	W	I	P	L
F	D	E	N	P	U	D	M	T	R	T	U	A	T	E	P
D	S	T	Y	L	S	A	R	C	Z	S	B	L	X	J	I
S	E	E	X	V	N	S	A	Y	R	R	U	D	I	D	C
E	H	M	T	Y	T	E	S	L	V	I	W	A	O	N	S
T	A	C	A	O	R	H	L	H	C	O	I	T	D	A	I
J	N	D	N	N	Y	T	U	U	E	T	S	U	M	E	N
P	Y	G	L	O	E	R	D	S	D	O	G	S	M	S	D
W	S	D	U	D	E	L	L	A	A	F	N	J	O	R	Y
C	M	T	H	G	W	E	R	E	M	J	R	H	C	K	E

Acts, chapter 19 verse 26b

Paul has persuaded and turned away a great many people saying that gods made with hands are not gods.

highlights from **ACTS ... chapter 19**

1 ACROSS: While Apollos was in Corinth, Paul was traveling through the inland country and arrived at Ephesus. He discovered that the disciples there had no knowledge of the Holy Spirit as they had only received John's B __ __ __ __ __ __. (Acts 19:1-3)

2 DOWN: He explained that John's was a baptism of repentance, telling people to believe in the one who was to come, Jesus. Hearing this, they were baptized in the name of the Lord. When Paul laid his H __ __ __ __ on them, the Holy Spirit came on them and they began speaking in tongues and prophesying. About 12 men in all were there. (Acts 19:4-7)

3 ACROSS: Paul remained there for three months, preaching Christ boldly in the synagogue. When some began speaking evil of the Way, Paul took the disciples to the hall of Tyrannus and reasoned daily with them there. He did this for 2 years, so that all the residents of Asia Minor heard the W __ __ __ of the Lord. (Acts 19:8-10)

4 DOWN: God used Paul in miraculous ways, even using handkerchiefs that had touched his skin, to heal the S __ __ __ and those possessed by evil spirits. When 7 sons of the high priest Sceva tried to copy him the evil spirit in a main said "Jesus I know, and Paul I recognize, but who are you?" chasing them from the house, wounded and naked. (Acts 19:11-16)

5 DOWN: News of this spread amongst the residents of Ephesus. Many believers publicly burned books of the magic arts, valued at about 50,000 pieces of silver. So the Word of the L __ __ __ spread widely and powerfully. (Acts 19:17-20)

6 DOWN: After these events Paul stayed in Asia Minor a while but sent T __ __ __ __ __ __ and Erastus ahead to Macedonia, resolving in the Spirit to pass through Macedonia and Achaia, before going to Jerusalem, and after that Rome. (Acts 19:21-22)

7 ACROSS: Around that time Demetrius, a silversmith, who made silver S __ __ __ __ __ __ for the goddess Artemis, gathered his fellow tradesmen together and stirred them up against Paul, saying that he was endangering both their trade and in fact the very worship of the goddess Artemis. (Acts 19:23-27)

8 DOWN: Enraged and shouting, "Great is Artemis of the Ephesians!", they dragged Gaius and Aristarchus, two of Paul's traveling companions, into the theatre. Some in the crowd prompted Alexander, a Jewish leader to speak, but when they realized he was a J __ __, they would not hear him and continued their chanting for about 2 hours. Meanwhile the disciples discouraged Paul from going to the confusion in the theatre. (Acts 19:28-34)

9 ACROSS: The town clerk eventually quieted the C __ __ __ __ saying, "We all know Ephesus keeps the temple of the great goddess Artemis and the sacred stone that fell from the sky. These men are not sacrilegious or blasphemers of our goddess. The courts are open, and the proconsul is there; if Demetrius and the tradesmen have a complaint let them bring charges. And if you are not satisfied, it shall be settled in the regular assembly. There is no justification for today's commotion, in fact we are in danger of being charged with rioting." And with those words he dismissed the assembly. (Acts 19:35-41)

(To be continued ...)

BAPTISM; HANDS; WORD; SICK; LORD;
TIMOTHY; SHRINES; JEW; CROWD

ACTS

Chapter 19

highlights from ACTS ... chapter 20

1 DOWN: After the uproar in Ephesus, Paul said goodbye to the disciples and departed for Macedonia, encouraging all as he went. He stayed there three months and had planned to sail to Syria, but discovering a plot A __ __ __ __ __ __ him, instead went back through Macedonia. (Acts 20:1-3)

2 ACROSS: A group went A __ __ __ __ to wait for us at Troas: Sopater, the Berean (he was Pyrrhus' son); Articus and Secundus, the Thessalonians; Gaius of Derbe; Tychicus and Trophimus from Asia Minor; and Timothy. (Acts 20:4-5)

3 DOWN: After the Feast of Unleavened B __ __ __ __, we sailed from Philippi to Troas for five days and stayed there seven days. On the first day of the week, we broke bread, intending to depart the next day, but Paul's sermon lasted until midnight. (Acts 20:6-7)

4 ACROSS: The U __ __ __ __ room where we met was on the third floor, and was lit with many lamps. A young man named Eutychus was sitting in the window. As Paul continued talking longer and longer, Eutychus sank into a deep sleep, and fell to his death. (Acts 20:8-9)

5 DOWN: But Paul went down, and took him in his arms saying, "Do not be alarmed, there is still life in him." They returned U __ __ __ __ __ __ __, broke bread, ate and talked till dawn. Then Paul left them comforted knowing Eutychus was alive. (Acts 20:10-12)

6 ACROSS: The rest of us set sail for Assos, but Paul went by land meeting us there. We sailed to Mitylene, reaching opposite Chilos the next day; touching Samos the next day; and the day after that Miletus. Paul was hurrying to J __ __ __ __ __ __ __ __, trying to get there in time for Pentecost, so he decided to sail past Ephesus. (Acts 20:13-16)

7 DOWN: The Elders from Ephesus met Paul in Miletus. He reminded them that he had not shrunk from preaching the G __ __ __ __ __ of faith in our Lord Jesus Christ, to both Jews and Greeks, in the public places and houses, despite plots against him. (Acts 20:17-21)

8 ACROSS: Paul told them he was going to Jerusalem, bound to do so by the Holy S __ __ __ __ __, knowing nothing more than that chains and tribulations awaited him there. But concern for his life would not deter him from finishing the course and the ministry given to him from the Lord Jesus. (Acts 20:22-24)

9 DOWN: He told the E __ __ __ __ __ that they would not see him again, so they must remember the whole counsel of God and must carefully conduct the duty given them by the Holy Spirit to oversee and care for the church of God. Paul warned them that men would arise, even from amongst their own number, twisting things, in an attempt to draw away disciples after them, so they should be alert. (Acts 20:25-31)

10 DOWN: He then commended them to God's G __ __ __ __; reminded them of his example of hard work to meet his needs and to be able to help those in need, honoring the Lord Jesus' words, "It is more blessed to give than to receive." Then they prayed together, sorrowfully embraced and kissed Paul, and accompanied him to the ship, knowing that they would never see him again. (Acts 20:32-38)

(To be continued ...)

AGAINST; AHEAD; BREAD; UPPER; UPSTAIRS;
JERUSALEM; GOSPEL; SPIRIT; ELDERS; GRACE

ACTS

Chapter 20

T O N I T M I R H C O E D R O L

R H B H B G U D E X C L H X U E

M G O A C E N L W N E A W O L Y

F S E L B A E I A O V U A T S I

E L E N U U S T I L R B L X J E

U E L V F G I A L J R D J I R C

S H S I L R H L C A Y B L D N R

E G P A E C E L D S G O M N G I

J N O H D R O C U E N E E A D U

S A N C T I F I E D O G V N V O

W I R N D H T I A F M N I D E Y

H W H L P S E S E C A R G C K E

Acts, chapter 20 verse 32

And now I commend you to God and to the Word of His Grace, which is able to build you up and give you an inheritance among all those who are sanctified.

D F A Q G Y R P Y D B U S D M N
R T V W B E O Y O X N Z N P F E
M N F R L H R G K D J A E C N L
F L U A P T V D A C H C R O I T
Q E T L S O E R E Z I Y D A H H
N E P I U N S K Y I B Z E I R I
D H N X T I F S J V F W N U L N
U I G U O R H T E A K I D Y A G
M V R N Y P R P U W S Q R T E S
J E F L F X J D E I O P P O S D
W D J H G U O R H T F M V X L O
C D L O H E S U O H E R S I H G

Acts, chapter 21 verses 19b to 20a

… Paul related one by one the things that God had done among the Gentiles through his ministry. And when they heard it they glorified God

highlights from **ACTS … chapter 21**

1 DOWN: We took our leave of the E __ __ __ __ __ from Ephesus, who met us in Miletus, and continued on our journey to Jerusalem. First setting off for Cos, and the next day Rhodes, and from there to Patara. Then we boarded a ship headed for Phoenicia, passed by Cyprus and landed at Tyre, Syria where the ship was to unload its cargo. (Acts 21:1-3)

2 ACROSS: The disciples at Tyre, through the Spirit, discouraged Paul from going on to Jerusalem. But he was not dissuaded so the men, their wives and children all accompanied us to the beach, where we K __ __ __ __ and prayed and then said good-bye. (Acts 21:4-6)

3 ACROSS: Our next stop for just a day was Ptolemais; then on to Caesarea where we stayed with Philip (one of 7 evangelist), who had 4 unmarried daughters who prophesied. While there, a P __ __ __ __ __ __ named Agabus visiting from Judea, bound his own hands and feet with Paul's belt and said, "Thus says the Holy Spirit, this is how the Jewish religious leaders in Jerusalem will bind the one who owns this belt." (Acts 21:7-11)

4 ACROSS: We all then urged Paul not to go to Jerusalem, but he answered, "Why are you weeping and breaking my heart? I am willing to even die in Jerusalem for the name of the Lord Jesus." He could not be P __ __ __ __ __ __ __ __, so we ceased and said, "Let the will of the Lord be done." (Acts 21:12-14)

5 DOWN: Accompanied by some of the D __ __ __ __ __ __ __ __ from Caesarea, we left for Jerusalem staying there at the house of Mnason of Cyprus, one of the first converts. They welcomed us warmly and the next day we met with James and all the elders. Paul related in detail all God had done through his ministry to the non-Jews. (Acts 21:15-20)

6 DOWN: They G __ __ __ __ __ __ __ __ God on hearing his report and then went on to tell him about the zealous Jewish believers who were spreading news that Paul was teaching Jews to abandon Moses law and customs such as circumcision. (Acts 21:21-22)

7 ACROSS: They suggested that Paul and four others take a vow of purification at the temple to show that as a Jew he lived in observance of the L __ __ of Moses; and that they send the letter with their judgement that non-Jews need only abstain from things strangled, sacrificed to idols, and from blood, and from sexual immorality. (Acts 21:23-26)

8 ACROSS: Paul's P __ __ __ __ __ __ __ __ __ __ __ days were almost completed, when the Jewish leaders seized him, repeating their accusation and stirring up the whole city against him. Word reached the Roman tribune, who at once dispatched centurions and soldiers, rescuing Paul from the mob by arresting him and binding him in chains. (Acts 21:27-34)

9 ACROSS: As Paul was about to be taken to the barracks he corrected the tribune's mistaken impression that he was an assassin, informing him that he was a J __ __ from Tarsus in Cilicia. The tribune granted Paul permission to address the crowd and Paul then switched from the Greek with which he addressed the tribune and began to address the people in Hebrew. (Acts 21:35-40)

(To be continued …)

ELDERS; KNELT; PROPHET; PERSUADED;
DISCIPLES; GLORIFIED; LAW; PURIFICATION; JEW

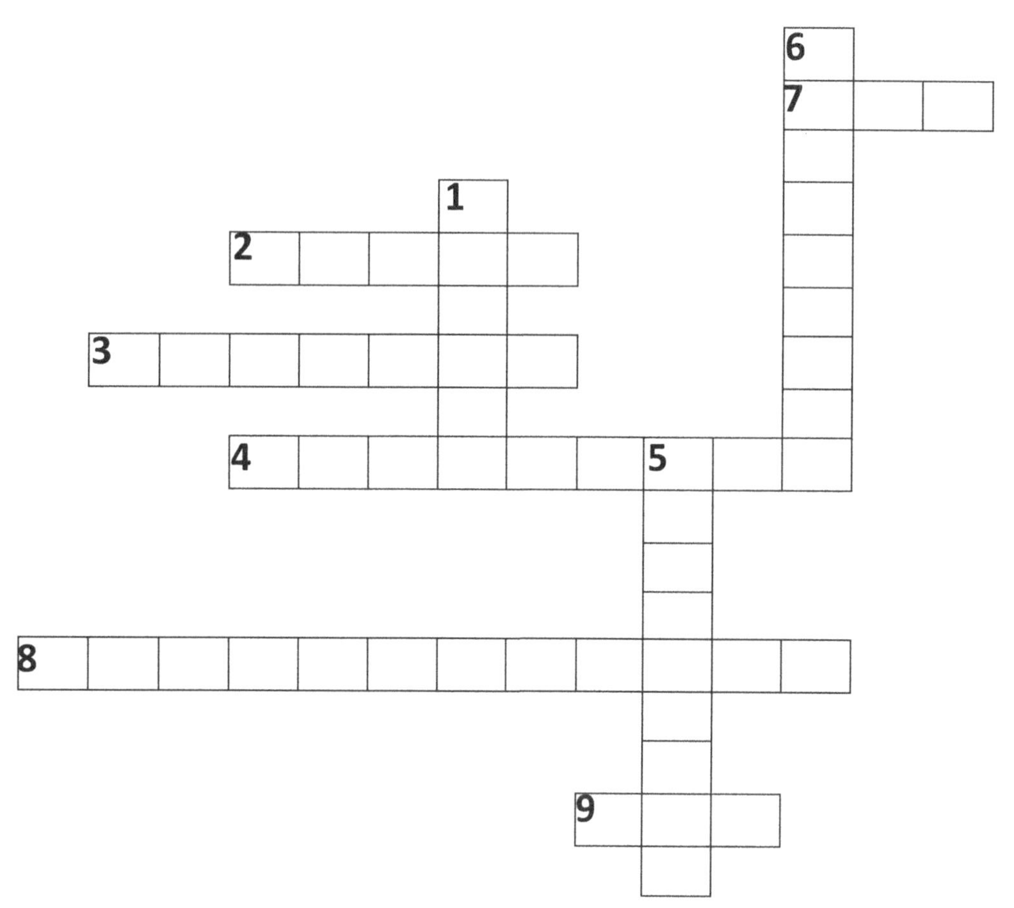

ACTS

Chapter 21

highlights from **ACTS … chapter 22**

1 ACROSS: In custody of the soldiers, and by permission of the tribune, Paul addressed the mob that had attacked him from the steps of the T __ __ __ __ __ in Jerusalem. He spoke in Hebrew saying, "Brothers and fathers, hear me" (Acts 22:1)

2 DOWN: The crowd became quiet, when they noticed that he was speaking in H __ __ __ __ __. Paul continued, "I am a Jew; I was born in Tarsus of Cilicia; I was brought up in this very city. I was educated in the strictest of manners, according to the law of our fathers, by none other than Gamaliel. (Acts 22:2-3)

3 ACROSS: I was as zealous for God as all of you are. I even persecuted the followers of this Way, binding and delivering both men and W __ __ __ __ to prison and even to death. The High Priest and the council of elders can verify what I'm saying. (Acts 22:3-4)

4 DOWN: I was on my way to Damascus with letters authorizing me to bring back more of them to Jerusalem to be punished. But as I got close to Damascus, at about N __ __ __, a bright light from heaven suddenly surrounded me, and I fell to the ground. The light was so bright that I lost my sight. (Acts 22:4-6)

5 DOWN: I heard a voice saying, 'Saul, Saul, why are you persecuting Me?' and I answered, 'Who are You Lord?' And He replied, 'I am Jesus of Nazareth, whom you are persecuting.' Those with me saw the L __ __ __ __, but did not understand the voice. (Acts 22:7-9)

6 ACROSS: I asked, 'What shall I do Lord?' and He said, 'Rise, go on to Damascus, and there you will be T __ __ __ all that you are to do.' In Damascus Ananias, a devout Jew met me saying, 'Brother Saul receive your sight' and immediately I could see. (Acts 22:10-13)

7 DOWN: Ananias continued, 'God has appointed you to be a witness for the Righteous One to all; and now get up, be baptized and wash away your sins, calling on His N __ __ __.' I returned to Jerusalem, and while praying in the temple I saw Jesus, in a vision telling me to 'Make haste, leave Jerusalem quickly because they will not accept your testimony about me. Go for I will send you far away to the Non-Jews.'" (Acts 22:14-21)

8 DOWN: On hearing this the C __ __ __ __ began to shout, "Away with this fellow; he should not be allowed to live!" The tribune ordered Paul back to the barracks to be examined by flogging, in order to find out why the crowd was shouting. (Acts 22:22-24)

9 ACROSS: When they stretched Paul out in preparation to be whipped, he said to the centurion standing nearby, "Is it lawful to flog an uncondemned Roman citizen?" The centurion brought the question to the tribune, saying, "Be careful what you are about to do for this man is a R __ __ __ __citizen." (Acts 22:25-26)

10 DOWN: The tribune immediately stopped the examination when P __ __ __ told him that he was a Roman citizen by birth. The next day he brought together Paul (unbound), and the chief priests and council to tell the real reason for the Jews' accusation. (Acts 22:27-30)

(To be continued …)

TEMPLE; HEBREW; WOMEN; NOON; LIGHT; TOLD;
NAME; CROWD; ROMAN; PAUL

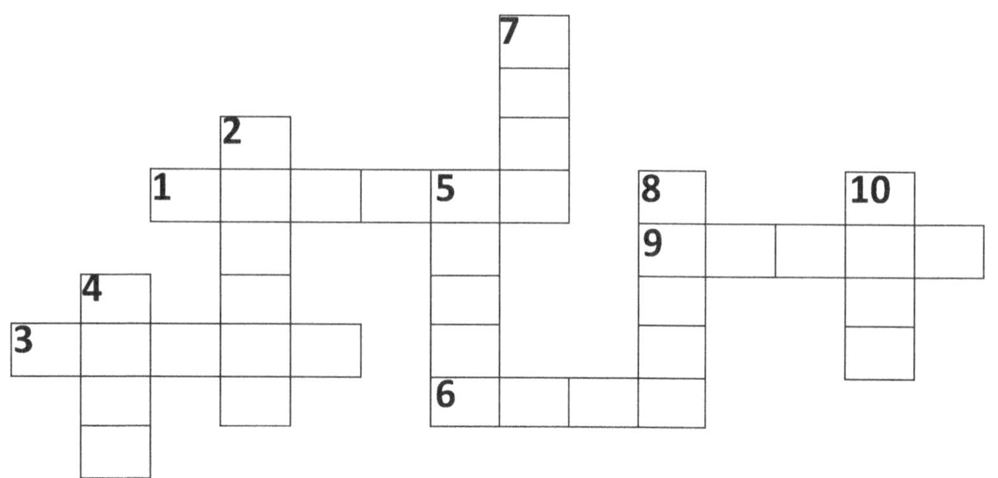

ACTS

Chapter 22

D S A Q G P W D H C N U N P S U

R F Y A W A S H E C E S V E D F

S E O R K L R B K D N A W X P O

F U B C I D A S A I T A H A E R

D G S D L P M O S G W B L M J Z

S O A E T S T A Y E N Z D I N P

E G R I J I E H L O F I L N L D

H A Z L E R W L R B U R L I A S

T E D Y S A T R U E Z R E L E D

D Y G B I X R D I J S G S G A N

W S D T R P I Q L S F N O X H C

C M T O G B A O E H T R S D K E

Acts, chapter 22 verse 16

And now, why do you wait? Rise and be baptized and wash away your sins, calling on His (Jesus) name.

Y F A Q G P W D H C N U N O S D
L S V E E M O R N I A M T X E F
E E F A K L V P A D E E A I P O
T U B N D A D S O L S A L T E T
A R T I Y W T R A T U B S X J O
E G A R U O C S I R R I O I N T
U S B T S C U F L V I W L N L U
C I C N C R I L E B G P L A A O
C S N B E E D R U T E L O R D B
A I G J D Y F I T S E T P M S A
W D F U L P L Q L S H S A O R A
C E Y L A T A R U E C A S N K E

Acts, chapter 23 verse 11

The Lord stood by him (Paul) and said, "Take courage, for as you have testified to the facts about me in Jerusalem, so you must testify also in Rome.

highlights from **ACTS … chapter 23**

1 ACROSS: The Roman tribune had taken Paul into custody. He then untied him and set him before the chief P __ __ __ __ __ __ and all the council. Paul then addressed them, "Brothers, I have lived my life before God in all good conscience up to this day. (Acts 23:1)

2 DOWN: Ananias, the High Priest, then commanded that he be struck on the M __ __ __ __, to which Paul responded, "God is going to strike you, you whitewashed wall! Are you going to command that I be struck, knowing it is contrary to the law." (Acts 23:2-3)

3 DOWN: When those nearby said, "Would you revile God's High Priest?" Paul responded, "I did not know he was the H __ __ __ Priest, for it is written, 'You shall not speak evil of a ruler of your people.'" (Acts 23:4-5)

4 ACROSS: Paul noticed that the council consisted of both Pharisees and Sadducees, so knowing the Sadducees say there is no resurrection, he declared, "Brothers, I am a Pharisee, and it is because of the H __ __ __ of the resurrection that I am on trial." (Acts 23:6-8)

5 DOWN: Things became violent, so the T __ __ __ __ __ __, afraid that Paul would be hurt, commanded the soldiers to get him back to the barracks. The following night the Lord stood by Paul and said, "Be courageous, you have testified of me in Jerusalem, and you must do so also in Rome." (Acts 23:9-11)

6 ACROSS: The next day, about 40 Jews vowed not to eat or drink till they had killed Paul. They went to the Jewish leaders with their plan to A __ __ __ __ __ and kill Paul as the tribune was bringing him for trial. But Paul's nephew heard of the plan and reported it to Paul who then sent him to the tribune. (Acts 23:12-18)

7 DOWN: The tribune questioned Paul's N __ __ __ __ __ privately and charged him to tell no-one of the details of their meeting. He then ordered two centurions to commandant 200 soldiers, 70 horsemen, and 200 spearmen along with mounts for Paul to ride, and to go by night to the governor Felix, as far as Caesarea. (Acts 23:19-25)

8 DOWN: They overnighted in Antipatris and the next day the H __ __ __ __ __ __ __ were sent on with Paul to Caesarea, while the others returned to the barracks. (Acts 23:31)

9 ACROSS: They delivered a L __ __ __ __ __ from tribune Claudius Lysias to His excellency, Governor Felix explaining that Paul, a Roman citizen, was being accused by the Jewish leaders in a matter of their law, and that he could find nothing in the matter deserving of death or imprisonment. (Acts 23:26-29)

10 DOWN: The letter went on to say that after discovering a plot to kill Paul, he sent him at once to Felix ordering his accusers to bring their case before the governor. On reading the letter and on discovering Paul was from Cilicia, the G __ __ __ __ __ __ __ commanded him to be guarded in Herod's praetorium until his accusers arrived. (Acts 23:30-34)

(To be continued …)

PRIESTS; MOUTH; HIGH; HOPE; TRIBUNE; AMBUSH;
NEPHEW; HORSEMEN; LETTER; GOVERNOR

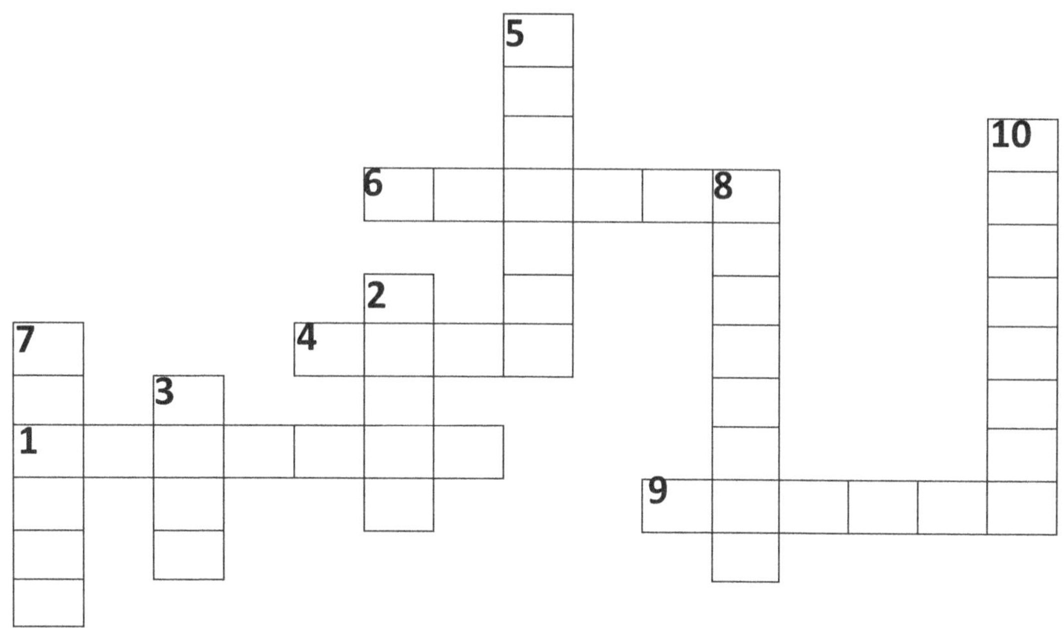

ACTS

Chapter 23

highlights from ACTS … chapter 24

1 ACROSS: Five days later Ananias, the High Priest, the elders, and Tertullus, the orator arrived at Caesarea, to present their case against Paul before Governor Felix. Tertullus began by saying: "Most Noble F __ __ __ __, by your foresight this nation enjoys great peace and prosperity, for which we are all thankful. Nevertheless, I beg that you graciously hear a few words from us and we will endeavor not to be tedious." (Acts 24:1-4)

2 DOWN: "We have found this man to be a plague, a creator of dissension, and a ringleader of the sect of the Nazarenes. He even tried to profane the T __ __ __ __ __. We seized him to judge him according to our law, but the Commander Clausius Lysias came, violently took him out of our hands, demanding we come before you." (Acts 24:5-9)

3 ACROSS: The G __ __ __ __ __ __ __ then gave Paul the nod to speak. So, he answered, "It is because I know that you have been a judge of this nation for many years, that I am moved to cheerfully answer for myself. You may ascertain for yourself that I had gone to Jerusalem to worship no more than twelve days before all this." (Acts 24:10-11)

4 DOWN: "During this time, they neither found me in the temple disputing with anyone or inciting the crowds either in the S __ __ __ __ __ __ __ __ __ or in the city. Nor can they prove any of their accusations against me." (Acts 24:12-13)

5 DOWN: "I worship the God of my fathers, believing all that is W __ __ __ __ __ __ in the Law and the Prophets, and I do so according to the Way, which they call a sect. I strive to live in good conscience toward man and God and like them, I too have hope in God that there will be a resurrection from the dead for both the just and the unjust." (Acts 24:14-16)

6 ACROSS: "I've returned to Jerusalem after many years to bring donations, and I was quietly in the temple. Certain Jews from Asia were also there and either they or even these men present today should now state what wrongdoing they saw in me. Unless of course they had a problem when I declared that "I am being J __ __ __ __ __ concerning the resurrection of the dead." (Acts 24:17-21)

7 DOWN: Felix, who already was quite familiar with the Way, adjourned the proceedings pending the arrival of Lysias. He commanded that Paul be G __ __ __ __ freedom for his friends to visit and to bring him whatever he needed. (Acts 24:22-23)

8 ACROSS: After some days Felix and his Jewish W __ __ __ Drusilla summoned Paul to address them concerning faith in Christ. Felix became fearful as Paul reasoned about righteousness, self-control and judgement, and dismissed him saying he would call on him again at a "convenient time." (Acts 24:24-25)

9 DOWN: Felix sent for Paul often in the hope that Paul would offer a bribe for his release. This continued for two years until Felix was replaced by Porcius Festus. Felix, as a favor to the Jews, left Paul as a P __ __ __ __ __ __ __. (Acts 24:26-27)

(To be continued …)

FELIX; TEMPLE; GOVERNOR; SYNAGOGUES;
WRITTEN; JUDGED; GIVEN; WIFE; PRISONER

ACTS

Chapter 24

S H T I S W I P H F N U N T D L

R A R A B N K R E X E L H X T U

M N I A K R E L E D L L W U P A

F D E N P A I M T R J Z O T E P

D S T Y S X A R C U S B L X J I

S J E O V N S A D R A Y D I D C

E H N T A T E G L V I W A O N S

T E C W O S E L F C O N T R O L

D N A N B M T D U E P S U M E N

P Y S S E N S U O E T H G I R D

W S D N D E L L A A F N J O S Y

C M T H G W E R E D E M R A L A

Acts, chapter 24 verse 25

When (Paul) reasoned about righteousness and self-control and the coming judgement, Felix was alarmed and said, “Go away for the present. When I get an opportunity, I will summon you.

T O N D T M I R H C O E O R D L
R H A H B G U D E X C L H X U E
M E L A C E N L T N S A W O L Y
D T U O B A E I U O V U A T R I
E L E N S U F T P L R P L X E P
U E L U F G T F S J R D I I L C
S Y S I L R H L I A Y B V D I R
P E E A E C E L D R G O E N G D
J N O H D R O C U E M E F A I U
S A N D T I F I E D O E V N O V
W I R N C H T I A F M N D Z N Y
H L U A P S E S E C A R G C K E

Acts, chapter 25 verse 19

… Rather they (the chief priests and leaders) had certain points of dispute against him (Paul) about their own religion and about a certain Jesus who was dead but whom Paul affirmed to be alive.

highlights from **ACTS … chapter 25**

1 DOWN: Festus, left Caesarea for Jerusalem, three days after his arrival in the province. While there the chief priests and leaders of the Jews urged him to bring Paul back to Jerusalem for trial. (They were planning to A __ __ __ __ __ and kill Paul on the way.) (Acts 25:1-3)

2 ACROSS: But Festus replied that he would soon be returning to C __ __ __ __ __ __ __ and that their leaders should accompany him. "If there is anything wrong about the man, let them bring charges against him." (Acts 25:4-5)

3 ACROSS: He stayed approximately ten more days before returning to Caesarea. The day after his return he took his seat on the T __ __ __ __ __ __ __ and ordered Paul be brought before him. The Jews who had accompanied him brought serious but unsubstantiated charges against Paul. (Acts 25:6-7)

4 DOWN: Then Paul spoke: "I have committed offenses neither against Jewish law, nor against the temple, nor against Caesar." But F __ __ __ __ __ wishing to do the Jews a favor said to Paul, "Do you wish to go to Jerusalem or to be tried before me?" (Acts 25:8-9)

5 DOWN: Paul replied "I have done no wrong as you well know. I appeal to Caesar." Then, after Festus had conferred with his council, he responded to P __ __ __ with, "To Caesar you have appealed; to Caesar you shall go." (Acts 25:10-12)

6 DOWN: Some days passed, and king Agrippa and Bernice arrived at Caesarea. Festus laid out Paul's case before the king. He explained that Felix, his predecessor had left Paul in prison; that the Jewish L __ __ __ __ __ __ wanted a sentence condemning him to death. (Acts 25:13-15)

7 ACROSS: But when they faced Paul at trial, they only had points of dispute about their own religion and about a certain J __ __ __ __ who was dead but whom Paul asserted to be alive. (Acts 25:16-19)

8 ACROSS: Festus continued by telling king Agrippa that he was at a loss as to how to investigate these matters and he had asked Paul if he wanted to return to J __ __ __ __ __ __ __ to be tried regarding them. But Paul had appealed for the decision of the emperor; and so, he was keeping Paul in Caesarea until he could be sent to Caesar. (Acts 25:20-21)

9 DOWN: Agrippa wanted to hear from Paul himself so Festus arranged a M __ __ __ __ __ __ for the next day. At the appointed time king Agrippa and Bernice entered the audience hall with great pomp, accompanied by military tribunes and prominent men of the city. At Festus command Paul was brought in. (Acts 25:22-23)

10 ACROSS: Festus then said "King Agrippa, and all present: the Jewish people have petitioned me to condemn this man to death but I have found that he has done nothing deserving of death. He has appealed to the E __ __ __ __ __ __ but it seems to me unreasonable to send a prisoner without indicating the charges against him. (Acts 25:24-27)

11 DOWN: I have therefore brought him B __ __ __ __ __ you all, and especially before you king Agrippa, so that after we examine him, I may have something to write. (Acts 25:26)

(To be continued …)

AMBUSH; CAESAREA; TRIBUNAL; FESTUS; PAUL; LEADERS;
JESUS; JERUSALEM; MEETING; EMPEROR; BEFORE

ACTS

Chapter 25

highlights from **ACTS … chapter 26**

1 DOWN: With King Agrippa's permission Paul began to speak: "I am so happy to be able to answer concerning all of which the Jewish leaders have accused me, especially because you, O King Agrippa, are an expert in J __ __ __ __ __ customs. Please be patient with me" (Acts 26:1-3)

2 ACROSS: "From my youth I have lived in Jerusalem, and if willing those here can testify that I was brought up as the strictest of Pharisees. And now king Agrippa I stand in judgement of my hope in the P __ __ __ __ __ __ made by God to our fathers." (Acts 26:4-7)

3 ACROSS: "Why does anyone think it is incredible that God raises the dead? Indeed, even I was so convinced in my opposition to the name of Jesus of Nazareth that I both imprisoned, persecuted, and participated in execution of the saints, and even journeyed to do so in Damascus authorized and commissioned by the C __ __ __ __ priests." (Acts 26:8-12)

4 DOWN: "As I travelled, at midday, a light brighter than the sun surrounded me and those with me. We all fell to the ground and I heard a voice addressing me in the Hebrew saying, 'Saul, Saul, why are you P __ __ __ __ __ __ __ __ __ __ me?'" (Acts 26:13-14)

5 ACROSS: "Who are you Lord? I asked. And the Lord said 'I am Jesus. Arise; you are to be a witness to your people and to the non-Jews, so that they may turn from D __ __ __ __ __ __ __ to light, from the power of Satan to God, to receive forgiveness of sins and a place among those who are set aside by faith in Me.'" (Acts 26:15-18)

6 ACROSS: "And so I obeyed the heavenly vision, declaring in Damascus, Jerusalem, the region of Judea and to the non-Jews that they should T __ __ __ to God in repentance. This is why the Jewish leaders seized me in the temple and tried to kill me." (Acts 26:19-21)

7 DOWN: "By God's help I continue testifying to both S __ __ __ __ and great of what Moses and the prophets said would come to pass: that the Christ must suffer, and by being the first to rise from the dead would proclaim light to all peoples." (Acts 26:22-23)

8 ACROSS: As Paul spoke Festus loudly declared, "Paul, you are mad; much learning is driving you out of your mind." But Paul responded, "No, most excellent Festus, I speak true and R __ __ __ __ __ __ __ words. King Agrippa knows of these things of which I speak. I know that you, King Agrippa, believe me." (Acts 26:24-27)

9 ACROSS: And Agrippa said to Paul, "Would you P __ __ __ __ __ __ __ me to be a Christian in a short time?" To which Paul responded, "I wish that all hearing me might be such as I am … except for these chains." (Acts 26:28-29)

10 DOWN: King Agrippa, Governor Festus, Bernice and all those sitting with them then withdrew. "This man deserves neither D __ __ __ __ nor prison" they said. King Agrippa then said to Festus, "He could have been set free, had he not appealed to Caesar." (Acts 26:30-32)

(To be continued …)

JEWISH; PROMISE; CHIEF; PERSECUTING; DARKNESS;
TURN; SMALL; RATIONAL; PERSUADE; DEATH

ACTS

Chapter 26

D F A Q G M R P Y D B U S D M N

R T V W O E O Y O X N Z N P U E

E S I R L H R G K D J A R C S L

F L F A P F T S I R H C E H T I

Q E T L S Z E R M Z I Y D A O G

N E P I U N S G Y I B Z E I R H

D H N X F K N S J V A W A D L T

U I G U F I H T E A K L D L A G

M V R N E P R P U W S Q C U E S

J E F B R X J S E I O P P O S D

W D J H G U O R T D F M V W R O

C D L O H E S U B H E R S I H P

Acts, chapter 26 verses 22b

… I (Paul) stand here testifying both to small and great saying nothing but what the prophets and Moses said would come to pass: that the Christ must suffer and that by being the first to rise from the dead, He would proclaim light both to Jews and Gentiles (non-Jews).

Y F A Q G P W D H C N U N O S D
L S V E E M O R N I A M T X E F
E T F A K G V H A D E E A I P O
P U B N D A D S E L S A L T E T
A R T I Y W T R G A U B S K J O
E G A R U O C S I R R I A I N T
U S B T S C U F L V I T L N L U
E I C N C R A L E B G P L A A O
C V N B K I D R U T E L O R D B
G I A J T Y F I T S E T P M S A
W D F H L P L Q L S H S F O R A
C E Y L A T A R U E C A S N K E

Acts, chapter 27 verse 25a

So take heart, men, for I have faith in God …

highlights from ACTS ... chapter 27

1 ACROSS: Paul and some other P __ __ __ __ __ __ __ __ were handed over to Julius, a centurion of the Augustan Cohort. Accompanied by a Macedonian from Thessalonica named Aristarchus they boarded an Adramyttium ship heading for ports along the coast of Asia Minor. The next day we put in at Sidon. (Acts 27:1-3)

2 DOWN: Julius treated Paul kindly allowing him to go and be cared for by his F __ __ __ __ __ __. On leaving Sidon, the winds were against us so we sailed across the open seas past Cyprus, along the coast of Cilicia and Pamphylia, coming to Myra in Lycia. (Acts 27:4-5)

3 ACROSS: There the centurion put us on an Alexandrian ship sailing for Italy. We had a slow and difficult number of days S __ __ __ __ __ __ to Cnidus. Sailing along the side of Crete that was sheltered from the wind we came to a place called Fair Haven. (Acts 27:6-8)

4 DOWN: The Fast holidays being over, we were now in the dangerous time for sailing. Paul advised them that sailing on would come with injury and loss of cargo, the ship and lives. But the C __ __ __ __ __ __ __ __ listening to the pilot and owner of the ship decided to sail on with hopes of wintering in Phoenix, a harbor of Crete. (Acts 27:9-12)

5 DOWN: A gentle south wind made them feel safe so weighing anchor they sailed alongside Crete, close to the shore. But soon they were being violently storm-tossed, caught in a northeaster, which drove them to a small I __ __ __ __ __ called Cauda; and so, they began to lighten the ship by throwing cargo and other things overboard. (Acts 27:13-19)

6 ACROSS: They abandoned all hope of being rescued as the tempest made it impossible to see neither sun nor stars. They had not eaten for a long T __ __ __ and Paul stood up and said, "You should have listened to me, but take heart there will be no loss of life, only loss of the ship. This very night, an angel of the God to whom I belong and who I worship, told me to not be afraid for I must stand before Caesar; and God has granted me all who sail with me. But we must run aground on some island." (Acts 27:20-26)

7 DOWN: On the fourteenth night the sailors tested the D __ __ __ __ of water they were in, and for fear of running against the rocks they let down four anchors and prayed for daylight. They tried to escape in the ship's boat, pretending they were lowering anchors, but Paul warned the centurion and the soldiers cut the ropes of the boat. (Acts 27:27-32)

8 ACROSS: At the sight of dawn Paul encouraged them all to eat and be strengthened, assuring them that none would perish and he took bread, gave T __ __ __ __ __ to God and began to eat. All 276 of them took courage, ate and then lightened the ship by throwing the wheat into the sea. (Acts 27:33-38)

9 DOWN: At daylight, they did not recognize the land, but noticed a bay and headed for it. They struck a reef and the ship began to be broken up by the surf. The soldiers, not wanting the prisoners to escape, wanted to kill them but the centurion, wishing to save Paul stopped them. Those who could S __ __ __ were ordered to do so and the rest to float in on planks or pieces of the ship. So, all were brought safely to land. (Acts 27:39-44)

(To be continued ...)

PRISONERS; FRIENDS; SAILING; CENTURION;
ISLAND; TIME; DEPTH; THANKS; SWIM

ACTS

Chapter 27

highlights from ACTS … chapter 28

1 ACROSS: We escaped the tempest to the safety of an island called Malta. The people welcomed us and built a F ___ ___ ___ to warm us from the rain and the cold. As Paul gathered sticks for the fire a viper came out of his bundle and fastened itself on his hand. (Acts 28:1-4)

2 DOWN: The local people seeing the S ___ ___ ___ ___ hanging from his hand thought that Paul must be a murderer who though he had escaped drowning, his fate must be to die for his crime. But when they noticed that he neither was swollen, nor did he die, they decided that he must be a god. (Acts 28:5-6)

3 DOWN: Publius, the chief man of the I ___ ___ ___ ___ ___, entertained us for three days at his nearby property. It so happened that his father was sick and Paul prayed, laid hands on him and healed him. Seeing this others came and were healed. (Acts 28:7-10)

4 ACROSS: After three months we left in a ship from Alexandria that had wintered there. We put in at Syracuse for three days, then made a circuit ending in Rhegium. The first day a south wind sprang up, and on the second day we arrived at Puteoli. The brothers there invited us to stay for S ___ ___ ___ ___ days before we travelled on to Rome. (Acts 28:11-14)

5 DOWN: When the brothers in R ___ ___ ___ heard about us they came as far as the Forum of Appius and the Three Taverns to meet us, and Paul thanked God and took courage. Paul was allowed to stay by himself along with the soldier guarding him. (Acts 28:15-16)

6 ACROSS: Three days later Paul called together the local Jewish leaders telling them that although he had done nothing against his fellow Jews or Jewish customs, he had been made a prisoner of the Romans in J ___ ___ ___ ___ ___ ___ ___ ___. "Seeing no justification for the death penalty they wanted to free me but the Jewish leaders objected and so I was compelled to appeal to Caesar." (Acts 28:17-19)

7 ACROSS: "And so" Paul continued, "I wanted to speak with you because I am in chains because of the hope of Israel." The Jewish leaders in Rome then said to him, "We have received no report about you, but we would like to H ___ ___ ___ your views on this sect that we know is spoken against everywhere." (Acts 28:20-22)

8 ACROSS: At the appointed day a great many of them came to Paul's lodgings where he expounded all day long about the K ___ ___ ___ ___ ___ ___ of God, convincing them about Jesus using the Law of Moses and the Prophets. Some believed and some did not. They left after Paul made the statement that the Holy Spirit speaking to their fathers through the prophet Isaiah had declared … (Acts 28:23-25)

9 DOWN: "This people's H ___ ___ ___ ___ had grown dull lest they should understand and turn and be healed." Paul continued, "Let it be known that this salvation of God has been sent to the non-Jews and they will listen." (Acts 28:26-29)

10 ACROSS: Paul lived there in Rome for two years at his own expense, welcoming all who came to him and boldly proclaiming the kingdom of God and T ___ ___ ___ ___ ___ ___ ___ about the Lord Jesus Christ. (Acts 28:30-31)

(To be continued …)

FIRE; SNAKE; ISLAND; SEVEN; ROME; JERUSALEM;
HEAR; KINGDOM; HEART; TEACHING

ACTS

Chapter 28

S H T I S W I T H O U T N T D L

R A R A G S E R S S E N D L O B

M N I A N N L L A M O D G N I K

F D E S I A I M C R J Z I T E P

D S E Y M X A H T O S M L X J I

S J T O I N S A C R M Y D I D C

E E N T A T E G L A I E A O N S

T S C W L S E L L C E N D R O L

D U A G C M T C U E P T U M E N

P S S F O N O U O E T H G I R D

E C N A R D N I H A F E J O S Y

C M T H P W E R E D E M R A L A

Acts, chapter 28 verses 30b and 31

(Paul) welcomed all who came to him, proclaiming the kingdom of God and teaching about the Lord Jesus Christ with all boldness and without hindrance.

Abiding in Christ

When Christians talk about work-life balance, Matthew chapter 16 verse 26, which says "What shall it profit a man if he gain the whole world and lose his own soul?" is often quoted. But, how does one not "lose one's soul"?

I'll begin with some background info. Genesis chapter 2 tells us that God put spirit in body and created man, a living soul. Genesis chapter 3 tells of the broken relationship between God and man. The rest of the Old Testament tells of man's futile attempts to restore that relationship as he tries to obey a series of ordinances and commandments.[1]

In the New Testament we see God, in His Grace, sending His Son[2]; for if we abide in the Son we will have the same relationship with God, the Father, that the Son has with Him. Man will be back home, no longer a lost soul.

Abiding in Christ means believing Jesus Christ, the Son of God, came to repair mankind's broken relationship with God. The cost of the repair: His death on the cross; the evidence of the repair: His resurrection...this is faith in the Gospel.[3]

Abiding in Christ demands returning control of one's soul to God; no longer my way, now Christ's way... this is repentance.[4]

Abiding in Christ requires immersing oneself fully in Christ; all that I am, body and spirit... this is baptism.[4]

Abiding in Christ means having the Holy Spirit living within, transforming through the Word, prayer, praise, fellowship, the giving of ourselves, aligning our will to the will of God, producing fruit of the Spirit... this is faithfulness.[5]

And so ... it is of profit when job, finances, possessions, life passions are all used in Abiding in Christ, ... being back home, no longer a lost soul.

Footnotes:

1. Acts chapter 13 verses 38 to 39: Therefore my friends I want you to know that through Jesus the forgiveness of sins is proclaimed to you. Through Him everyone who believes is set free from every sin, a justification you were not able to obtain under the law of Moses.
2. John chapter 3 verse 16: For God so loved the world, that He gave His only Son that whoever believes in Him should not perish but have eternal life.
3. 1st letter to the Corinthian Christians, chapter 15 verses 1 to 4: Now brothers and sisters, I want to remind you of the Gospel I preached to you … by this gospel you are saved, if you hold firmly to the word I preached you. Otherwise you have believed in vain. For what I received I passed on to you as of first importance: that Christ died for our sins according to the scriptures, that he was buried, that he was raised on the third day according to the scriptures …
4. Acts chapter 2 verses 36 to 38: "God has made this Jesus whom you crucified, both Lord and Messiah". When the people heard this they were cut to the heart and said to Peter and the other apostles, "Brothers, what shall we do?" Peter replied, "Repent and be baptized every one of you, in the name of Jesus Christ for the forgiveness of your sins."
5. Romans chapter 15 verse 13: May the God of hope fill you with all joy and peace as you trust in Him, so that you may overflow with hope by the power of the Holy Spirit.

Made in the USA
Columbia, SC
22 January 2024

30808243R00096